# TRADITIONS OF DEATH AND BURIAL

## Helen Frisby

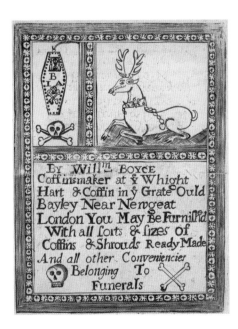

SHIRE PUBLICATIONS

Bloomsbury Publishing Plc

PO Box 883, Oxford, OX1 9PL, UK

1385 Broadway, 5th Floor, New York, NY 10018, USA

E-mail: shire@bloomsbury.com

www.shirebooks.co.uk

SHIRE is a trademark of Osprey Publishing Ltd

First published in Great Britain in 2019

© Helen Frisby, 2019

Helen Frisby has asserted her right under the
Copyright, Designs and Patents Act, 1988, to be
identified as Author of this work.

A catalogue record for this book is available from the
British Library.

ISBN: PB 978 1 78442 377 3

    Ebook 978 1 78442 380 3

    Epdf 978 1 78442 378 0

    XML 978 1 78442 379 7

19 20 21 22 23   10 9 8 7 6 5 4 3 2 1

Typeset by PDQ Digital Media Solutions, Bungay, UK

Printed and bound in India by Replika Press Private Ltd.

## COVER IMAGE

Front cover: A skull and crossbones form a poignant
*memento mori* atop a tomb. Back cover: Lilies are
traditional funeral flowers. (Sergey Urzhumskov/CC
BY 2.0)

## TITLE PAGE IMAGE

Trade card (*c.*1680) of William Boyce of Great Old
Bailey, Newgate, London, the first recorded undertaker
in England. Boyce's shop was named 'Ye Whight Hart
& Coffin' (see page 32).

## CONTENTS PAGE IMAGE

Woodcut funeral scenes, *c.*1850, featuring horse-drawn
hearses and mutes carrying crape-covered wands.

## ACKNOWLEDGEMENTS

I am more grateful than words can express to all those
family, friends and colleagues who have trodden this
journey with me. Particular thanks go to Russell
Butcher at Shire for all his help and infinite patience;
also to Dr Brian Parsons, Professor Hilary Grainger
OBE and Dr John Rumsby for kindly sharing images
from their personal collections. Many organisations
and companies also have generously allowed me to use
images from/of their collections. Yasmin Al Rehani,
Brigid Hewett, Sam Watts and Nicolas Wheatley have
all been wonderfully supportive, and especial thanks
are due to Dr Terri Sabatos and to my writing buddy
Lin Lovell. Mum and Dad have always supported and
encouraged my research interests, however off-beat, and
helped by taking photographs. This book is especially
dedicated to Andy, my husband and best friend who has
over the years become more accustomed to living with
death than anyone should have to.

Images are acknowledged as follows:

Alamy, page 10; Bakewell PCC, page 28; Birmingham
Conservation Trust/Coffin Works, pages 58 and 59;
Birmingham Library, page 60; British Library, London,
UK/© British Library Board. All Rights Reserved/
Bridgeman Images, page 5; ©The Trustees of the British
Museum. All rights reserved, page 1; Crazy Coffins Ltd,
page 77; The Cremation Society of Great Britain, page
50; Getty Images, pages 6, 13, 16, 26, 43, 56, 57, 64,
70, 72, 74, 75, 79; Professor Hilary Grainger, page 66;
iStock, page 87; Hugh Llewelyn, page 18 (bottom);
Metropolitan Museum of Art, New York, page 45;
Motorcycle Funerals Ltd, page 78; Dr Brian Parsons,
pages 61, 63, 63, 83; by permission of the Pepys Library,
Magdalene College Cambridge, page 27; Resomation
Ltd, page 82; Dr John Rumsby, page 53; Victoria and
Albert Museum, London, page 41; Wellcome Collection,
pages 8, 24, 29, 30 , 31, 39, 40, 49 (bottom), 51; Yale
Center for British Art, pages 3, 22, 32, 34, 47 (top), 55;
York Castle Museums Trust, page 52.

All other images are the author's own.

Shire Publications supports the Woodland Trust, the
UK's leading woodland conservation charity.

# CONTENTS

# INTRODUCTION: THE DEATH OF DYING?

W E'RE ALL GOING to die; but it's become the great
unmentionable. Despite the physical comforts of
modern Western life, the process of dying has somehow
become socially, spiritually and emotionally impoverished.
This book will explore how ordinary English people since the
Middle Ages onwards have faced up to the inevitable, and
what we might be able to learn from the past about dealing
with death and dying.

In particular this book explores how, through the medium
of custom and tradition, relationships between the living, the
dying and dead have been shaped and reshaped over the last
millennium. In some cases, the outward form of these customs
and traditions has changed dramatically over time, reflecting
changes in society, culture and technology. That said, there
are also certain funeral customs and traditions which have
changed little, and which our medieval ancestors might well
recognise. And (nearly) always, echoing down the centuries
to the present day and looking ahead to the future, there has
been that powerful underlying need for connection with the
dead – loved and hated ones to be sure, but also our own
future dead selves.

There is one brief but significant exception to this. By the
1990s the impact of two World Wars, followed by a half-
century of particularly fast, deep social and cultural change,
seemed finally to have severed relations between the world of
the living and that of the dead. The dead, however, are patient.

Indeed, it was just as the late-twentieth-century death taboo appeared most firmly established, that new funeral customs and traditions were already emerging. Furthermore, many of these 'new ritualisations of death', as they are often called by academics who study the history of funerals, often turn out under closer examination to be modern twists upon centuries-old, tried and tested customary forms.

This story of how the English have related – or not – to their dead over almost a millennium is told here in five chronological chapters. The second chapter covers the period from *c*.1066 to 1500, during which relationships between the living and the dead were driven by high and sudden patterns of mortality. Through an entire raft of popular customs and beliefs, the living could gain both emotional satisfaction and social status by assisting the dead in their post-mortem journeys through Purgatory. In the process one could also gather spiritual credit to ameliorate one's own future progress when the time came.

High and sudden mortality also characterised the early modern period (*c*.1500–1750), which is the subject of the third chapter. The official abolition of Purgatory by Protestant reformers undoubtedly impacted the nature and extent of relationships between the living and the dead. However, other evidence gathered by antiquarian and folklore collectors of the time points us toward a complex story of public conformity,

Angels conduct the spirits of benefactors into Heaven, the portal of which is opened by St Peter for their reception, while below, two saints watch a contest between St Peter and Satan for a soul at the Last Judgement. Both images extend across two pages of the New Minster Liber Vitae.

Fifteenth-century Doom painting in Holy Trinity Church, Coventry. At a time when death often came suddenly, and few could read, such vivid depictions of the after-life reminded people to be prepared for death at all times.

yet also private resistance to change in this regard. The latter part of this period saw social and technological changes including the rise of the middle classes and beginnings of modern medicine, which would later come greatly to reshape the process of dying.

It was during the next, industrial period (fourth chapter, *c*.1750–1900) that modern, urban consumer culture really began to influence English deathways. That said, not only did the older notion of connectedness with the dead persist in popular custom, but the products of modern mass manufacture themselves became imbued with the magical ability to assist and relate to the dead. Again, the story of death in English custom and tradition is complicated and often surprising.

Despite the death toll of the 1914–18 Great War, as recounted in the fifth chapter (*c*.1900–2000) many Victorian and older funeral customs and beliefs could still be found in England well into the inter-war period. The introduction of the Chapel of Rest during the 1930s would, however, prove a key development. Along with the arrival of the motor hearse around the same time, this eventually rendered many previous funerary customs redundant. This willing abandonment of tradition in favour of practical convenience highlights an important point: that many of the older customs had been emotionally and financially burdensome, not to mention socially intrusive and physically unpleasant. This reminds us that the line between history and mere nostalgia is a fine, but important one when it comes to death and funeral traditions. The decades following the Second World War would see the ascendancy of this kind of 'practical death' as rapid social changes – especially in the role and position of women – took effect.

Almost a quarter of the way through the twenty-first century, however, and it's clear that dying has life in it yet. For most British people, death nowadays is the predictable conclusion of a long life – although modern lifestyle habits may be changing this. When it does eventually come, twenty-first-century death is usually caused by the chronic diseases of extreme old age. Arguably this kind of death presents its own social, emotional and spiritual challenges, meaning that the need for funeral customs and traditions remains as powerful as ever. Perhaps we will only stop needing to relate to the dead if and when we as a species finally achieve immortality – at which point, it could be said, we cease anyway to be human.

Some of the historic and present-day customs and traditions discussed in the following chapters will seem so obvious and mundane as to be almost unworthy of comment; while others may feel alien, even shocking. All, I hope, will in their own way make you think and talk about what mortality means to you. Most of all, however, I hope that reading about and considering death in custom and tradition will encourage us all to think that little bit more about what it means to live.

# THE PAINS OF PURGATORY, c.1066–1500

I F FUNERAL CUSTOMS and traditions emerge and endure because they get the deceased to where they need to go, and the bereaved where they need to be, then during the Middle Ages it was above all the Christian concept of Purgatory which afforded these needs ritual shape. The shadowy, fragmented nature of the evidence from the early part of this period in particular means that much remains unknowable concerning the specifics of what happened at the deathbed and afterwards. Where evidence does exist it often describes the customs and experiences of elite individuals rather than the common people, so a degree of inference must be made. However, we do know that by the mid-1200s there was established the general notion that the dead, their souls caught in the cosmic battle between good and evil, and facing the judgement of God himself, could and should be assisted on their way by the living. Underlying this was the idea, comforting and burdensome in doubtless equal measure, that the relationships between the dead and living might be enduring even beyond the grave.

This idea would become formalised and elaborated into the doctrine of Purgatory, as adopted by the Second Council of Lyons in 1274. Unlike the soul's final destinations of Heaven and Hell, Purgatory was the intermediate place where souls went to be cleansed of their venial (forgivable) sins committed in life. Medieval theologians and artists often depicted Purgatory as being more like Hell than Heaven, insofar as the

OPPOSITE
*Ars Moriendi* or, in this case, how not to die. This illustration (c.1503) depicts a restless man on his deathbed, with looming demons ready to take his soul. Dying badly could undo the effect of a lifetime of good works, condemning a person to a difficult passage through Purgatory – or even to Hell.

cleansing was by way of fiery torment. Unlike Hell, however, Purgatory offered the prospect of eventual redemption and ultimately passage to Heaven. The next logical step was to assume human agency; that there were things people could do to help themselves and others have a shorter, easier time in Purgatory. In particular, one could accrue spiritual credit in this life by performing good works and then dying a good death when the time came.

In fact, if anything a good death was most important: it might redeem a life of all but the worst sin, whereas a last-minute slip of behaviour could undo an otherwise impeccable lifetime of virtue. While the concept of the embattled post-mortem soul dated back to Anglo-Saxon times, these increasingly high stakes led to the emergence of the concept of the *ars moriendi*, 'the art of dying'. Deathbed scenes in later medieval pamphlets and paintings, sculpture and stained glass, repeatedly show the dying person as lucid and serene, surrounded by family and friends. This ideal probably gained all the more imaginative power by contrast with the grim reality of sudden death from infectious disease or accident, with little hope nor pain relief. A series of demographic disasters and associated social upheaval during the 1300s – widespread famine from 1315–17, the

Line drawing of an image from the Lisle Psalter entitled 'The three living and the three dead.' In this medieval *memento mori* poem, three kings out hunting meet three walking corpses who, as it transpires, are their ancestors now suffering in Purgatory for indulgences in life.

Black Death of 1348–49, then further plague outbreaks in 1361 and 1369 – only rendered these big questions of life, death, judgement and salvation even more urgently fearful.

Given death's swiftness and lack of discrimination, it was essential that everyone should be prepared for the inevitable. This required knowledge of the physical signs of approaching death, such as those listed in John Reynes' commonplace book:

Whanne mine ehynen misten
And mine eren sissen
And my nose koldeth
And my tunge foldeth
And my rude slaketh
And mine lippes blaketh

Such was the widespread fear of unexpected death and being caught out in a bad moment and consequently dispatched straight to Hell, that people looked anywhere they could for death portents. According to *The Owl and Nightingale* (*c*.1250) 'men be of the owl sore afraid; who singest ere some man shall be dead', a folk death portent belief still being recorded in 1930s Lincolnshire. The medieval folk death portent belief that the number of a cuckoo's cries portended the years of life left also endured well into modern times.

Having disposed of material properties and made provision for prayers to be said for their soul via a will, the final step of the good death was to receive the last rites. When summoned the priest would attend, saying the seven penitential psalms as he made his way to the deathbed. On arriving he would sprinkle the dying person with holy water, and a crucifix would be held in front of them while prayers including the Lord's Prayer were said. If possible there followed an examination of the dying person's belief in the central tenets of Christianity, and their confession was heard. Although *in extremis* – and especially during the Black Death – a dying person might make confession to a layman, this was not ideal, and in 1511 people in the diocese of Canterbury complained to the authorities there that the dying were missing out on these vital ministrations, due to absent or otherwise unavailable priests. Finally there came absolution, by anointing with holy oil on the eyes, ears, nostrils and mouth, the loins or back, and the feet. Such was the finality of this Extreme Unction, there existed a strong lay belief that one who did recover after receiving it lived a limbo existence thereafter, forbidden from eating meat or having sex.

During these critical moments before, during and immediately after death, the living could also assist a soul on its way by having the passing-bell rung. This was believed to protect the vulnerable soul from airborne demons, while being yet another *memento mori* for the living. There were special patterns to the ringing, which varied from neighbourhood to neighbourhood but usually identified the age and sex of the deceased.

Immediately after death the body was washed, shrouded and laid out, a task invariably carried out by women. Gregory's *Dialogues* (*c*.AD900) is an early attestation that the dead were cared for in this manner. Beyond its obvious practical functions, symbolically the shroud protected the dead person and recalled their baptism. As the sermonist John Mirk noted, it advertised that they were 'clean shriven and cleansed of [their] sins' and therefore deserving of a quick and easy passage through Purgatory. Meanwhile for the bereaved, this act of washing and dressing the body would have afforded comfort as a final gesture of spiritual and physical care. Illustrations from the 1450s onwards indicate a variety of shroud wrapping, pinning, sewing and knotting techniques. Gregory refers to embalming as a foreign practice, and we know from later sources that flowers, sweet herbs and sometimes spices were employed to mask the smell of decay. In the case of Dr John Caius, joint founder of the eponymous Cambridge college, who died in 1573, 'spice and sweet powders for the corpse' cost no less than six shillings and eightpence (equivalent to almost £80 in modern terms). Rosemary and yew continued to hold particular folkloric associations in this respect well into the industrial period.

Until the mid-twentieth century, when the dead stopped being laid out at home, family, friends and neighbours would gather to watch over, or 'wake' the body the night before the funeral to protect it, both physically and spiritually. Candles helped ward off evil spirits, as did salt placed in and around the body. Perhaps the body's presence, with its natural processes of decay that begin immediately after death, also helped the bereaved accept the reality of events, to comfort one another and bond through the shared experience of grief. That said, social anthropologists have long observed that, as well as sadness, these occasions also usually involve confronting death through defiant jollity. From the earliest written sources we know that this was indeed the case in England, with Ælfric of Eynesham's *Life of Swithin* urging priests to abstain from the eating, drinking, 'heathen songs and loud laughter' of the laity at such gatherings. The oftentimes revelrous nature of the medieval funeral wakes is glimpsed again in 1535, with

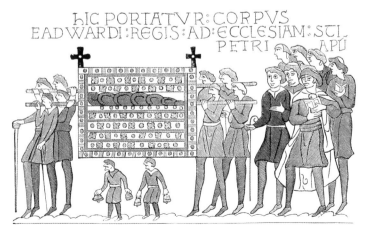

Funeral of St Edward the Confessor, 1066, as depicted in the Bayeux Tapestry. Note especially the handbells being used both to clear a path and frighten evil spirits away.

R. Olyver of York feeling obliged to specify in his will that there be 'no revel of young folks' at his wake. Both Ælfric and Olyver were, however, rare exceptions to a firmly established English tradition, a tradition moreover recurring – and invariably criticised by religious and other authorities – down the centuries.

Prior to the arrival of Christianity in the seventh century, a mixture of disposal by burial and cremation had prevailed. By the time of the Norman Conquest, the practice of burial in and around the church building had become established – as had the charging of fees for this privilege. Thus there arose the requirement to get the deceased where they needed to go in the most practical, as well as the spiritual sense. Coffins, sometimes repurposed containers and otherwise specially made, were used to contain the body during the journey. From the remotest moorland villages, it might take the bearers several days to manhandle their large, heavy and increasingly unpleasant burden, carried at waist height upon a hand bier, along the customary 'corpse road' to the parish church. Meanwhile in the growing towns funeral processions became showier as the Middle Ages progressed, as the guilds played an increasing role in putting on a good funeral show for and by their members. Guilds were confraternities, membership of which was by subscription and defined by common professions or religious interests – including in being remembered and prayed for after one's death. One of the guilds' main functions in medieval England was to ensure a good send-off for deceased members, and members could even be fined for failure to swell the crowd at a fellow member's funeral. In this sense, guilds might even be seen as distant, indirect ancestors of the Victorian burial club, and through them the modern life insurance industry. By emphasising the popularity and good standing of the deceased in this life, dramatic funeral processions with their black palls and costumes, bells (believed to scare evil spirits away), banners and hired mourners offered comfort to the bereaved beside soliciting the all-important prayers for the departing soul. In a study of wills from medieval Bury St Edmunds, testators from the 1490s onwards began to show an interest in, and take control of, their own funeral arrangements. For instance, of the seven who specified the colour of the mourning garments to be worn, six chose black – which had by now become the conventional mourning colour – but one stipulated russet. Some testators also mandated the number of poor people, whose intercessions were thought especially efficacious, to participate in their funeral processions, John Baret (d.1463) specifying five rather than the customary sixteen. Thus individual preference can already be seen beginning to nip at the strictures of convention.

During the Middle Ages – and well beyond – it was traditional for food as well as gloves, stockings and shoes and other items of clothing, together with cash from the deceased's estate, to be distributed to the assembled mourners. In addition to helping the soul pass over, the passing-bell would have been a signal for the local poor to assemble in anticipation of the dying person's last benefactions. The donors were motivated by more than simple generosity; by answering the cries of the poor for one last time they would have hoped to gain additional spiritual merit, through the prayers of the recipients, in order to help see them through the travails of Purgatory.

Until the Reformation there was no one, standard order of funeral service in England. Surviving liturgies such as those from the Old Sarum and Old York Missals indicate that the priest typically met the funeral party at the lych (its name possibly derived from Old English *licce*, 'corpse') gate, with the service then conducted in church. This usually took place over two days, beginning with the service of *Placebo* the evening before the main funeral mass. The following day's proceedings began with the priest marking out the grave in the shape of a cross then blessing the (usually) east-facing grave with holy water. During the requiem mass itself the body was surrounded by lit candles and censed in an anti-clockwise circle. Following the mass it was taken outside and laid, usually shrouded but un-coffined, into its grave. The priest pronounced absolution, the words of which were also written onto a parchment scroll and placed onto the corpse's breast. Willow or hazel staffs ('metewands'), symbolic of the Resurrection, might be placed in the grave, as might a small lead or wax mortuary cross. The priest cast earth onto the body, sprinkled it with holy water then censed it once more; then the commendation was read while the grave was closed. The great fourteenth-century theologian Thomas Aquinas opined that this elaborately ceremonial burial was beneficial for all concerned: for the dead who could no longer help themselves gain salvation; and as a *memento mori* ('remember death') for the living to be sure to accrue spiritual credit while they still might.

The practice of charnelling, whereby bones were exhumed and stored so that graves could be reused, was common in England beyond the Middle Ages.

After the ceremony a 'dole' of money, customarily a penny, together with food was normally distributed to the mourners present. The food often amounted to a meal, usually also held in the church or churchyard. Not only was this sharing of food and drink an opportunity for social bonding among the living, it was yet another means of securing the community's prayers for the deceased now in Purgatory. The effect was ideally reinforced, if of course funds permitted, by periodic memorials: 'minds' (typically seven and/or thirty days after burial); and annual 'obits'. Late medieval wills sometimes specify the food and drink to be provided at these events. This would have been as plentiful as the testator could possibly afford, and the items listed regularly included bread, beer, cheese, meat, game and spices. In a clear display of medieval priorities John de Crakell of York (d.1395) left £1 10s (£920) to pay for his funeral food – but only £1 (£610) to his daughter Joanna.

While burial in earth was the standard means of bodily disposal, the presence or absence of grave markers expressed and perpetuated social status even in death. For most ordinary people, the concept of permanent burial and commemoration remained many years in the future. Their grave markers, where they existed at all, would have been simple, perishable items, their decay on the surface mirroring that of the body inside the grave. Archaeologists have occasionally come across wooden cruciform memorials from this period, although such finds are rare. After a few years these bodily remains would often have been removed and stored carefully in charnel houses, and the grave re-used. All in all, churchyards in the Middle Ages were not exactly sacred places of remembrance and contemplation. Church statutes from Anglo-Saxon times onwards repeatedly – and unsuccessfully – attempted to curb secular activities within churchyards, which included animal grazing, food storage, sports, dancing, theatricals and markets. Perhaps it was therefore just as well that medieval relationships

OVERLEAF, TOP Memorial brass to William Hancok (d.1485) and his wife Ellen, inscribed 'Orate pro anima' – 'pray for the soul of', St Michael's Spurriergate, York (now the Spurriergate Centre).

Caption on previous page.

Tomb and effigy of William Canynges the Younger (d.1474), St Mary Redcliffe, Bristol. Wealthy merchant, MP, five times Mayor of Bristol and finally priest, Canynges put his fortune to work after his death, reaching out to the living for their prayers for his soul.

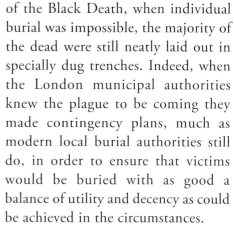

of mutual comfort and assistance with the dead did not necessarily require the grave as a physical focus.

Obviously the church liturgies portray ideal practices, but archaeological finds reveal that medieval burials do tend to have been placed with deliberate care. Even at the height of the Black Death, when individual burial was impossible, the majority of the dead were still neatly laid out in specially dug trenches. Indeed, when the London municipal authorities knew the plague to be coming they made contingency plans, much as modern local burial authorities still do, in order to ensure that victims would be buried with as good a balance of utility and decency as could be achieved in the circumstances.

Instead of burial with the masses in the churchyard, the wealthy could usually afford indoor ('intramural') burial within the church, and often a more permanent memorial in stone or brass calling for prayers ('*Orate pro*

*anima…*'). Such memorials could range from a relatively modest engraved brass plate attached to the nearby wall, to a fully life size, brightly painted effigy. The effigy as a form of commemoration is first seen in the eleventh century, an early example being the tomb of Abbot Gilbert Crispin of Westminster (d.1117/18). From this developed the transi, or cadaver tomb, in an especially dramatic attempt to grab sympathetic attention – and of course prayers – from the living. In addition to the normal lifelike effigy, the deceased was also represented as a cadaver complete with bones and worms. The decomposing cadaver could also be depicted in brass engraving.

From the mid-thirteenth century onwards the very wealthy took the logic of Purgatory – and also of individualism – yet another step further by constructing and endowing their own personal chantry chapels. Often these were established within existing churches – Lincoln Cathedral had no fewer than thirty-six of these by the time of the Reformation – although they might sometimes be standalone. Within the chantry a priest, sometimes more

John Wakeman, Abbot of Tewkesbury 1531–39, and later Bishop of Gloucester. Wakeman was eventually buried at Forthampton, Gloucestershire, but his cadaver tomb – complete with carved vermin representing the sins of the dead – lives on in the Abbey as a vivid *memento mori*.

Chantry chapel built c.1535 by Thomas West, 9th Lord de la Warr of Boxgrove, West Sussex. Heraldic devices are combined with Book of Hours motifs. Unusually, the 'pray for the soul of' inscription on its altar is in English rather than Latin. The chantry was never actually used due to the Reformation.

than one, would be employed to say constant masses for the founder. Having lost several of his family to plague in 1349, William Wakebridge of Crich, Derbyshire, must have been especially anxious on this point, for he founded two chantries, one dedicated to Saints Nicholas and Catherine (1350) and another to St Mary (1368). Wakebridge also contributed to the foundation or maintenance of another six chantries before his own death.

It was furthermore possible – money permitting, of course – to buy one's beloved dead remission from Purgatory through purchase of a Papal Indulgence. While in theory, then, death was the great leveller, in practice worldly social and economic distinctions absolutely were carried over into the next life. For those of more modest means, bequests of items for the church and/or an entry upon the parish bede roll were the usual mechanisms by which people secured an ongoing presence in the memories, and therefore the prayers, of the living. In the eleventh century, conscious that access to salvation was already becoming heavily determined by financial means, Abbot Odilo of Cluny (d.1049) founded All Souls' Day, or Soulmas, so that 'all the dead, who have existed from the beginning of the world to the end of time' might receive assistance from the living by means of prayer regardless of worldly means. Originally observed in February, All Souls' was soon changed to the day after All Saints', a move that eventually gave rise to many aspects of the modern Hallowe'en. John Mirk's *Festial* records the custom of giving food and alms to the poor on Soulmas Day, in exchange for their prayers for the needy souls in Purgatory. This particular custom gave rise to the traditional saying, 'a Soule-cake, a Soule-cake, Have mercy on all Christen soules for a Soule-cake.' Bells would be rung to accompany a formal requiem mass for the parish dead, together with a procession around the churchyard and blessing of the graves.

Since the early days of Christianity it had been accepted that ghosts existed and were a legitimate way for the dead to communicate with the living. Even authorities such as St Augustine acknowledged their existence. Although some medieval ghosts were simply vengeful, many were more concerned with the completion of unfinished business, and especially with having wrongs corrected on their behalf to enable them to rest in peace. In the Byland Tales, written around 1400 by an anonymous monk of the Yorkshire abbey there, the ghost of an excommunicated man sends Snowball the Tailor to York to obtain absolution for his sins. That the dead were believed capable of returning and communicating illustrates how ongoing relationships between them and the living transcended the boundaries between their

Wakefield Bridge chantry chapel (1342–56) is one of only four surviving bridge chapels in England. After the Reformation it was variously used as a warehouse, office and even a cheese shop. The original west façade was removed in 1832 and the current one dates from 1939.

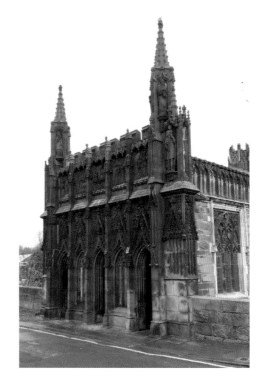

*What's Humane Life, Where Nothing Long Can Stand? Time Flyes, Our Glory Fades, and Death's at Hand.* Print by William Faithorne (1656–c.1701) illustrating the fragile, transitory nature of life and the inevitability of death.

respective worlds. It was not until after the Reformation that ghosts would become reinterpreted as demonic visitations.

Another variety of medieval living death was that of the leprosy sufferer. Their flesh rotten like that of a corpse, the leper was regarded as already in Purgatory, thus an adapted funeral was needed ritually to separate them from the properly living. First the leper was led into church by a priest chanting the seven penitential psalms. Confession, absolution and a mass followed, after which the leper was taken into the churchyard and earth thrown over their feet in a symbolic burial. From then on they were considered spiritually and socially dead, and 'passed over' into the separated space of the leper hospital.

Lepers at least received some form of funeral; a calculated absence or inversion of the normal funeral customs awaited the suicide, however. Unceremonious burial at night, and in un-consecrated ground, was mandated for those convicted of *felo de se*. Later on the Church began allowing suicides to be buried in churchyards, albeit at the north side traditionally associated with the devil, alongside other outsiders such as strangers and the un-baptised. 'Profane' burial could also include driving a stake through the body in order to prevent the ghost walking. This latter practice was still very occasionally recorded as late as 1775, when the corpse of a Captain Bolton, who had killed himself at York Castle while awaiting execution for murder, was roughly interred at three lane ends nearby and a stake driven through his heart in the presence of the castle turnkeys.

Prior to 1274, funeral customs increasingly embodied a growing assumption that humans possessed spiritual, social and emotional agency in the face of mortality: that there were things the living could do to and for the dead to assist them into the after-life. After 1274, and especially in the wake of the Black Death, the living and dead became bound up more tightly than ever into a reciprocal 'moral economy' of salvation. Death acquired an ever-stronger imaginative power, expressed through elaborate funeral customs and traditions and their associated material and visual culture. While occasional hints of individualism can sometimes be found in relation to funeral customs and tradition, in general medieval funeral customs and traditions are often alien and unsettling to twenty-first-century sensibilities. This is largely because they were the products of a time when morbidity patterns, coupled with the rudimentary nature of medicine, meant that death could strike anyone, anywhere, anytime and often with little warning.

As the sixteenth century dawned, Catholic popular piety seemed vigorous and well established. However, it was at this point that a challenge arrived from the continent, one that would steer English funeral customs and traditions off down a new path. Just how new and revolutionary that path really was, is the subject of the next chapter.

# The Diseases and Casualties this Week.

| | |
|---|---|
| Imposthume | 1 |
| Infants | 7 |
| Kingsevill | 1 |
| Mouldfallen | 1 |
| Kild accidentally with a Carbine, at St. Michael Woodstreet | 1 |
| Overlaid | 1 |
| Rickets | 9 |
| Rising of the Lights | 2 |
| Rupture | 2 |
| Scalded in a Brewers Mash, at St. Giles Cripplegate | 1 |
| Scurvy | 4 |
| Spotted Feaver | 2 |
| Stilborn | 13 |
| Stopping of the Stomach | 11 |
| Suddenly | 1 |
| Surfeit | 7 |
| Teeth | 27 |
| Tissick | 12 |
| Ulcer | 1 |
| Vomiting | 1 |
| Winde | 1 |
| Wormes | 1 |

| | |
|---|---|
| Abortive | 2 |
| Aged | 32 |
| Bleeding | 1 |
| Childbed | 5 |
| Chrisoms | 9 |
| Collick | 1 |
| Consumption | 65 |
| Convulsion | 41 |
| Cough | 5 |
| Dropsie | 43 |
| Drowned at S Kathar. Tower | 1 |
| Feaver | 47 |
| Flox and Small-pox | 15 |
| Flux | 3 |
| Found dead in the Street at Stepney | 1 |
| Griping in the Guts | 15 |

|  | Males | 121 | |  | Males | 195 | |
|---|---|---|---|---|---|---|---|
| Christned | Females | 111 | | Buried | Females | 198 | Plague 0 |
|  | In all | 232 | |  | In all | 393 | |

Decreased in the Burials this Week —————— 69

Parishes clear of the Plague —— 130    Parishes Infected —— 0

The *Assize of Bread* set forth by Order of the Lord Maier and Court of Aldermen
A penny Wheaten Loaf to contain Eleven Ounces, and three
half-penny White Loaves the like weight.

# REFORMATION AND RESISTANCE, c.1500–1750

SUDDENLY IN THE 1530s, the comforting mechanism of Purgatory was swept away by the Protestant Reformation. The practice of Indulgences as a way of helping the dead through Purgatory proved a particular touchstone for religious reformers such as Martin Luther and John Calvin. They emphasised instead the role of personal faith in securing post-mortem salvation. The Calvinist form of Protestantism that came to dominate in England espoused the doctrine of so-called 'double predestination.' This meant not only that God had already determined who was destined to be saved, but also who was to be condemned to Hell. So there was no longer any point in praying for the dead. Indeed, to do so was almost blasphemous, implying as it did a questioning of God's judgement. Purgatory, together with its associated ritual apparatus, was redundant.

In England the Reformation furthermore became inextricably entwined with King Henry VIII's twin political needs at that time. The first of these was urgently to remarry and get an heir, while the other was to finance ongoing conflicts with France and Scotland, money he obtained by quickly dissolving the English monasteries. The result was a Reformation largely imposed from above for political purposes, rather than – as in most of the rest of North-Western Europe – one grown upward from popular conviction. This engendered a peculiarly English disjunction in terms of funerary customs between law and lore, between official and popular beliefs and

OPPOSITE
Weekly Bill of Mortality for London, 21–28 February 1664. 'Aged', 'found dead in the street' and 'suddenly' are all listed as causes of death during a rare plague-free week.

'The Pestelence
1665' –
anonymous
illustration from
*Pepys' Diary* of
plague dead
being buried at
St Giles without
Cripplegate,
London. Present-
day burial
authorities are
still required to
have epidemic
mass body
disposal plans.

practices. The 39 Articles, the founding doctrinal statements of the new Church of England, unequivocally denounced Purgatory as 'a fond thing, vainly invented.' However, it would take more than strong words to dismantle Purgatory and its associated ritual apparatus, providing as these did a valued social, emotional and spiritual framework in the face of an otherwise unrelentingly bleak, judgemental cosmos.

Accordingly the period covered by this chapter witnessed discernible shifts in the public aspects of death, dying and remembrance, such as the funeral liturgy and tombstones. This period also saw the emergence of an urban middle class, which demanded the funerary accoutrements previously preserved for the wealthy, such as individual coffins and memorials, and individualism gathered pace in death as in life. However, there are also hints of a more complex story of private resistance to Protestant ideas about death and dying, with evidence that certain medieval funerary customs adapted and persisted.

It was also during this early modern period that Bills of Mortality first began to be produced. These were lists of deaths, with causes where known, in the preceding week, month or year. Although many of the 'causes' given were simple descriptions such as 'aged', some broad patterns are discernible. Infants and the elderly were most vulnerable during winter, when airborne respiratory diseases are most prevalent. Overall deaths peaked in March and April, presumably in the crossover period between these and the summer gastro-enteric diseases. Although never again on the scale of the Black Death, plague remained a perennial visitor and the 1665–66 outbreak has gone down in popular memory as especially virulent.

London suffered especially badly; rapid urbanisation without corresponding sanitary infrastructure was opening up a divide between urban and rural experiences of death and dying. Maternal and child mortality remained high, with London's infant mortality rate an especially horrifying one in three.

While information was one thing, medicine's ability in practice to manage mortality remained limited. Despite advances in the later half of the period, notably the discovery of smallpox vaccine, it remained imperative to be prepared for death. Death portent beliefs recorded at this time include the appearance of yellow spots on one's hand (1612), bees swarming onto dead wood (1714), a swallow falling down the chimney (1652), finding a spot on a mutton shoulder-bone (1586), a 'winding-sheet' in the candle-wax (1708) or 'coffin' shaped cinders in the fire (1727). In 1608, Katherine Foxegale of Walesbie (Walesby) was presented to the magistrates at Retford 'for watching upon Saint Markes even at nighte laste in the Church porche to presage by divelishe demonstracion the deathe of somme neighbours within this yeere.' This account is striking in several respects: firstly because it shows somebody actively seeking out a death portent; secondly the manner how, within the new Protestant scheme of things, interaction with the dead was now – quite literally – demonised; and finally because it exemplifies how magical thinking persisted alongside the newer scientific approach to death and dying.

When compared to the typical medieval deathbed *memento mori* literature, such as Jeremy Taylor's *Rules of Holy Dying*, it seems that less spiritual, social and emotional pressure was placed upon a person's

Clarke of Bodnam deathbed scene, illustrating the continued ideal of a good death into the early modern era. Pepys Ballads I 48.

Baby George Manners wrapped in a shroud secured at the feet with a twisted length of cloth: detail from Manners Tomb (1623), All Saints Church, Bakewell, Derbyshire. This method and style of shrouding was common during the seventeenth century.

final moments as the seventeenth century progressed. While the ideals of calm self-awareness and settling one's affairs remained, there was more sympathetic acknowledgement of the practical realities of dying. Pain relief, usually opiate-based, increasingly featured at deathbeds as the period progressed. It remained customary to make one's will upon one's deathbed, and surviving mid- to late-sixteenth-century wills from York evince a general shift in belief from Catholic (requesting prayers for the testator's soul and invoking the saints) to Protestant (bequeathing the soul to God's grace) sentiments in this respect. However, this was a protracted shift over several decades, rather than an immediate change. Even by the turn of the seventeenth century, a significant proportion of these York wills remain studiedly neutral as to whether the living might still pray for the dead.

That many people still believed it possible and desirable for the living to assist the departing soul is also suggested by the continued tradition of ringing the passing-bell when a person died. This was despite official attempts to curtail this particular custom and replace multiple rings with a single toll at the time of death; appointed Archbishop of York in 1570, Edmund Grindal repeatedly complained of its persistence, especially in the remoter areas of his vast Archdiocese.

Although a few extreme Puritans viewed the body as a 'stinking karkass' to be disposed of as mere rubbish, for most people the bodies of the dead were still something to be cared for and treated with dignity. French tourist Henri Misson (1719) described how typically, after the body had been checked for plague and its orifices stopped, women washed the body before dressing it in a long shirt that was then tied at the feet. A cap covered the head and fastened beneath the chin, holding the jaw shut, then gloves completed the outfit. If the body meantime failed to stiffen then, it was widely believed, this portended a further death in the household. This particular folk belief was still being recorded well into the industrial period. More pragmatically the government, recognising an opportunity to boost the woollen trade, passed the Burial in Wool Acts (1666, 1678 and 1680) which required the grave-clothes to be made from wool upon pain of a fine. To further disguise the effects of decomposition and maintain individual identity, bran in the coffin

soaked up bodily fluids, while bay, rosemary and other scented herbs helped mask the smell.

The treatment of criminal corpses highlights by contrast these prevailing norms regarding physical care for and of the dead. Legislation passed in 1540, 1565 and 1663 permitted the medical schools only six executed corpses a year between them for dissection, as doctors' curiosity about the workings of the human body increased. To have one's body treated in this manner, which went directly – and deliberately – against the norm of caring for the dead continued and compounded the criminal's punishment, even after death. This legal supply proved insufficient to meet the rapidly growing demand for anatomical subjects, however, and by 1750 there was a growing trade between the medical schools and the so-called 'resurrectionists' (colloquially known as 'sack 'em up men'), who made a living by exhuming newly buried bodies and selling them by the foot to the medical schools.

On a practical level, then, keeping and watching the dead at home prior to the funeral was a perfectly sensible

Two men placing the shrouded corpse which they have just disinterred into a sack while Death, as a nightwatchman holding a lantern, grabs one of the grave-robbers from behind. Coloured drawing by T. Rowlandson, 1775.

A coffin containing the body of Moll Hackabout surrounded by so-called mourners and the parson. In this engraving William Hogarth satirises behaviour at working-class wakes, from Moll's child sitting under the coffin playing with a top while dressed in mourning, to the parson spilling his drink. From *A Harlot's Progress*.

precaution to protect the body from such nefarious uses. However, the custom of waking also retained most of its earlier social, emotional and spiritual functions. Antiquarian John Aubrey recorded 'mimicall playes and sportes' still commonly taking place at funerals in the 1680s, together with drinking, tobacco-smoking, card games and prayers said knelt by the corpse. Especially suggestive of a continued sense that the dead required help into the after-life was the custom whereby, in exchange for a fee, food and drink were passed over the body in its coffin to a 'sin-eater'. By then consuming the food and drink the sin-eater absorbed the sins of the deceased, allowing his or her spirit to proceed unburdened. It is unclear whether this was an older medieval tradition, or an adapted form of Holy Communion transposed from the post-1552 funeral service into the home. Interaction between the newly dead and still-living could run both ways, with belief in corpse cures being widely recorded by Aubrey and others. There was also the popular belief that a murdered corpse would bleed afresh in the presence of its murderer.

The practice of embalming did not become the norm until many years later, so it was usual during this period for funerals to be held more quickly than nowadays. Surviving parish registers reveal that funerals were typically held within three to four days of death. In the affluent London parish of St Mary Woolnoth in the 1600s, for example,

Funeral ticket dated 1 July 1809, depicting a funeral procession entering a church. Etching by T. Cook after W. Hogarth.

70 per cent of funerals were held within three days, and 90 per cent within four days of death. Indeed, in summer 1624 a vicar from Cornwall was prosecuted for permitting a body to go unburied for three days in hot weather conditions.

With the funeral service now much reduced, the gathering of mourners beforehand acquired much greater social, emotional and even spiritual significance. This may help explain why some people – particularly the urban middle and upper classes – during this period began to restrict attendance at funerals by means of invitations, often in the form of a printed ticket. Food and drink would be served to the gathered mourners: Misson noted how it was 'usual to present the guests with something to drink, either red or white wine, boil'd with sugar and Cinnamon, or some such Liqor.' Along with this 'burnt wine' might be served sweet biscuits or cakes – those at well-to-do funerals often being of the fashionable Naples or Savoy variety, and including exotic ingredients such as almonds, rose-water, musk or ambergris. From the 1660s onwards the fashion was spreading to the provinces – at a funeral in Halifax in 1673, the mourners were sustained by cake and wine while they waited no less than five hours for the funeral to begin.

Ribbon slide commemorating the death of 'F.E.' in 1698 and converted into a ring during the twentieth century. An ivory skeleton set on plaited hair wields a scythe and hourglass, both symbols of mortality.

As with all funeral hospitality, the custom fulfilled multiple functions: refreshment for those who had travelled, social bonding and emotional comfort. Some historians have also suggested it may have been a vestige of the old funeral mass, another pre-Reformation funeral tradition now transposed into the domestic realm of folklore.

As manufactured goods became cheaper and more plentiful, gifts to mourners of gloves and hatbands, black ribbons and scarves became increasingly common. Mourning rings, ribbon slides and occasionally even spoons, might also be given at the funerals of the well-to-do. The growing urban middle classes also increasingly demanded individual coffins, coffin furniture and other funerary accoutrements such as weepers and plumes, black mourning cloaks, candles, palls, and hearses. Previously these had been restricted to the aristocracy, but as the College of Heralds' power to regulate these material distinctions of death was decisively broken by the sheer weight of demand there emerged paid professionals who 'undertook' the arrangements for the entire funeral ceremony. The first documented of these 'undertakers' is William Boyce of London, who from around 1675 traded from his premises 'at Ye Whight Hart & Coffin' near Newgate (see image on page 1).

For most ordinary people during this period the hired parish coffin and bier remained the normal means of transport to the graveside. Bearers were selected as far as possible to mirror the age, sex and marital status of the deceased, with children often bearing children's coffins; it was not unknown for pregnant women to bear the pall (a fabric cover over the coffin) at the funerals of women who had died in childbirth. A particularly striking instance of this mirroring was the 'bride's burial' of unmarried women, where women dressed in white carried their sister to the grave along with a 'virgin's crown' or 'virgin's garland'. Approximately a foot in height, the distinctive beehive-shaped wooden frame was colourfully decorated with coloured ribbons and paper flowers, and white paper gloves hung in the centre. In a merging of wedding and funeral symbolism, it was carried either before or on the coffin in procession, and later hung within the church; the earliest known surviving example, at St Mary's in Beverley, Yorkshire, dates back to around 1680. Literary references to the custom date back further, notably in Act 5 scene 1 of *Hamlet* (*c*.1610) where the priest says of Ophelia:

> Yet here she is allowed her virgin crants [crowns],
> Her maiden strewments and the bringing home
> Of bell and burial.

Maiden's garland, St Mary's Church, Alne, North Yorkshire. Probably nineteenth century, but made to a design dating back to at least the Tudor period.

After around 1700 the custom began to attract disapproval from the church authorities, and it became more common for the garland to be buried with the coffin rather than being displayed. However, documentary references and surviving examples are still found going into the nineteenth and even twentieth centuries, and the last recorded instance of this ceremony is at the funeral of Miss Joy Price of Ashford-in-the-Water, Derbyshire, in 1995.

Many of these folk customs appear to have arisen, or at least become considerably more prominent, as the

A Poor Man's Burial (1704). Note the presence of women and children in this working-class funeral procession. Several mourners carry sprigs of herbs, probably rosemary.

Reformation progressively stripped from the official funeral observances any reference to continuing bonds between the dead and the living. England's first national prayer book, the 1549 *Book of Common Prayer*, removed the *Placebo* and all use of candles and incense. Prayers and psalms were retained, although with the emphasis now on commending the soul to God. Communion was made optional. Shortly afterward in 1552 the Communion and psalms were completely removed from the funeral service, together with the commendation and any remaining hint of prayer for the dead. This recasting of the burial service from an act of care and assistance toward the soul to a more functional disposal of the body, reached its apogee with the 1645 *Directory for the Publique Worship of God*. Now a minister need not even be present at funerals, and if he happened to be, his primary role was to ensure the deceased was buried without so-called superstitious abuses. While many reformers recognised the funeral bell's value as a *memento mori*, there were – largely unsuccessful – attempts to limit its ringing to one peal only during the service. Altogether therefore, the Reformation removed any active role within the funeral service for the bereaved, with no prayers to be said nor ritual gestures to be made. Decency did, however, allow for 'civil respects or deferences […] appropriate to the rank and condition of the party deceased' to be paid. Funeral sermons, emphasising the status and virtues of the deceased in life, also became increasingly popular.

Seemingly then, funerals were becoming more secular and life-focused during this period. That said, there are intriguing hints on record that the old need and desire to perpetuate a connection with the dead persisted. Aubrey recounts the Lyke Wake Dirge, which depicted the deceased moving through the very physical, distinctly Purgatorial landscape of Whinney-moor in order to reach its destination. Indeed, Aubrey's version explicitly mentions Purgatory:

This ean night, this ean night,
every night and awl
Fire and Fleet and Candle-light
and Christ receive thy Sawle.
When thou from hence doest pass away
every night and awl
To Whinney-moor thou comest at last
and Christ receive thy silly poor sawle.
If ever thou gave either hosen [hose] and shoen [shoes]
every night and awl
Sitt thee down and putt them on
and Christ receive thy sawle.
But if hosen nor shoon thou never gave nean [none]
every night and awl
The Whinnes [thorns] shall prick thee to the
bare bean [bone]
and Christ receive thy sawle.
From Whinny-moor that thou mayst pass
every night and awl
To Brig o' Dread thou comest at last
and Christ receive thy sawle.
From Brig of Dread that thou mayest pass
no brader [broader] than a thread
every night and awl

To Purgatory fire thou com'st at last
and Christ receive thy sawle.
If ever thou gave either Milke or drinke
every night and awl
The fire shall never make thee shrink
and Christ receive thy sawle.
But if milk nor drink thou never gave nean
every night and awl
The Fire shall burn thee to the bare bene
and Christ receive thy sawle.

Here – unlike in the reformed funeral service – the soul is directly addressed and its fate clearly linked to its deeds in life as it is sent on its way. In these respects the Lyke Wake Dirge recalls both the medieval practice of prayers for the dead, and the old association between charitable works and the soul's posthumous salvation. The precariousness ('no brader than a thread') of its route to the after-life is also emphasised. Aubrey recorded the Dirge as still being performed by 'certain women' who would attend especially for this purpose, at Yorkshire funerals in the 1610s. Indeed, it would take a concerted campaign by churchmen during the eighteenth century and beyond finally to eradicate it from use altogether.

Another continued tradition was the distribution of doles after the funeral service. The post-funeral 'drinking' did however relocate from the churchyard after the Reformation, usually to the home of the deceased. In bequeathing £6 (£800) for refreshments at his funeral, yeoman Robert Waughe (d.1612) of Chester-le-Street described this provision as 'my last faire well [to family, friends and neighbours] out of this synfull world.' Although Waughe does not explicitly request any prayers for his soul, this wording implies that he is still the host to whom the recipients owe sympathy and gratitude. Waughe's largesse was not unusual in scale; if anything, the importance of the after-funeral meal actually increased following the Reformation, with food and drink now often accounting for half or more of the total funeral expenditure. Undertakers' bills show that meat and game, cakes and sweets, dried and fresh fruits, almonds, spices and other exotic confections were regularly served at the funerals of the affluent during this period. Pauper funerals paid by the parish sometimes included refreshments – typically bread, cheese and beer – while even in the cases of debtors the money was often found for a good send-off. So far as can be judged from the evidence, even the Civil War and Great Plague had little effect on the scale of funeral hospitality. The Protestant reformer Thomas More had claimed that funeral refreshments were nothing more than mere frivolous indulgence; clearly, however, the English disagreed.

Skull detail on a seventeenth-century tombstone at Elmore, Gloucestershire. Such devices would have functioned as a *memento mori*, reminding passers-by of the deceased and their own mortality.

The wearing of special mourning clothes beyond the funeral, a poignant symbol of the mourner's continued bond with the dead person, also began to gain popularity around this time. From around 1670 onwards, mourning fabrics such as black crape (or crêpe) are increasingly listed in drapers' inventories. While the custom was initially confined to court and aristocratic circles, as weaving and dyeing techniques improved it came increasingly within the financial reach of the affluent, aspirational middle classes. However, it was not until the 1820s that Samuel Courtauld finally perfected the manufacturing process, making mourning-wear accessible even further down the social scale.

For those who could afford a permanent tombstone, these memorials now emphasised the achievements, virtues and family relationships of the deceased in life, rather than soliciting prayers for the after-life. In other respects the medieval *memento mori* tradition persisted in the form of carved skulls, cross-bones and other stark reminders of mortality. Most ordinary people, however, continued to be buried in unmarked graves in their local churchyard, although archaeological evidence indicates an increasing use of individual coffins further down the social scale. Even during the major plague outbreak of 1665–66 the majority of the dead were still buried in an orderly fashion, in the traditional east–west orientation and avoiding the north side of the churchyard. This latter taboo persisted despite the increasing overcrowding in urban churchyards as the population grew; by as early as 1590, some London parishes were already having to buy land beyond the parish for new burials.

As chantries were the most public expressions of the old scheme of Purgatory and prayers, it is unsurprising that following Henry VIII's 1534 Act of Supremacy, they quickly fell out of use. While the bede roll entries tail off more slowly over the following years, there is nonetheless a very marked decline in their use after 1540, and the annual readings ceased. Candles and incense were also frowned upon. Altogether these sounds, sights and smells, which had kept alive spiritual, emotional and social bonds between the living and the dead, were systematically being removed from the public sphere. Royal Injunctions of 1536 and 1547, together with exhortations in the *Book of Common Prayer*, redirected the money toward more 'this-worldly' concerns in the form of poor relief. Yet again, however, the historical record hints tantalisingly at some degree of private resistance. In 1612, for instance, sixteen women and two men were accused of praying for the dead at crosses in the Yorkshire villages of Dishforth and Thornton-le-Beans. Further south, in Oxfordshire, and just over a century later, Richard Lydall's bequest of a bell loft and bell to the parish church of Northmoor in 1714 was accompanied by a request that the ringers pray for his soul.

While the Reformation in theory stripped away Purgatory and its associated ritual apparatus, by way of replacement it offered only the terrifying prospect of immediate, personal judgement before God with neither agency nor respite. It is therefore not surprising to find that the customs and traditions that had given the bereaved the comforting sense of still being in touch with the dead lingered, and in some cases, were adapted and reinvented. While the official funeral liturgy was now firmly for the bereaved, the dead were still popularly felt to have needs too; thus this period saw a divergence between official and 'folk' practice in relation to the dead.

This is not to say that funeral traditions stood totally still during this period. In fact the shape and pace of English society was changing profoundly, and such changes were inevitably expressed in death as well as in life. In particular this 'early modern' period witnessed the rise of an urban middle class whose members demanded the funeral accoutrements traditionally reserved for the nobility – the elaborate processions, the mourning-wear, the big memorials. This increasing demand for funeral trappings, further and further down the social scale, created a market, and the end of this period saw the emergence of the first dedicated funerary professionals. The undertaker had arrived.

*Undertakers In At The Death.* Death and money have had an uncomfortable relationship since the birth of the modern funeral industry. Coloured etching by R. Newton, 1794.

# DYING IN THE INDUSTRIAL AGE, c.1750–1900

IN TERMS OF how industrial modernity affected relationships with the dead, we can divide this period roughly into two. The period from around 1750 to 1850 was characterised by rapid population growth: from 6 million in 1741 to 8.9 million in 1801, then to 18.9 million by 1851. This rising population was also increasingly concentrated: whereas in 1801 only 20 per cent lived in towns of 5,000 people or more, 54 per cent were urban dwellers by 1854. Just ten towns accounted for around a quarter of the population, many of which had mushroomed in the midlands and north of England with little accompanying sanitary infrastructure. Thus when infectious diseases such as cholera, typhoid, typhus, diphtheria and influenza struck, these spread rapidly and the resulting mortality rates were high. Infant mortality

*The dance of death: the nursery. The lettering reads 'Death rocks the cradle: Life is o'er: the infant sleeps, to wake no more.' Infant mortality remained high until the 1910s, up to one in five in the poorest city districts. Coloured aquatint by T. Rowlandson, 1816.*

would also continue to be very high (certainly by present-day standards) throughout this entire period.

Exacerbated also by the increasing expectation of permanent, individual burial, the old urban churchyards were by now struggling to accommodate the sheer volume of burials. In 1839 George Alfred Walker commented how he had witnessed mourners slipping on exposed, decomposing flesh at a London funeral. 'Graveyard George' was one of several campaigners including Charles Dickens, who during the mid-nineteenth century agitated for the simplification and modernisation of English funeral custom and tradition. Rosary Road Cemetery in Norwich, opened in 1821, was England's first non-denominational 'garden cemetery'; it was followed by the Liverpool Necropolis, opened in 1825. Carefully laid out and planted with trees and shrubs, this new type of cemetery was a deliberate counterpoint to the unpleasantness of the old urban churchyards. They were also commercially run, a model that the government of the day wished to encourage; however by the 1840s it was clear that more decisive action was required to resolve the urban burial problem. The result was the Cemeteries Clauses Act, 1842, which provided for the foundation of local Burial Boards. These were empowered, at the local ratepayers' expense, to establish and maintain cemeteries, and this model of localised public burial provision endures into the present day.

The mid-nineteenth century also witnessed attempts to implement urban sanitary infrastructure such as drainage. Thus patterns of morbidity started gradually to change, so that fewer people died in young adulthood and of acute

*Fading Away*, 1858. Composite photograph by Henry Robinson of a young woman dying of tuberculosis. This particular illness was romanticised by the Victorians as a 'good death'.

infectious disease. The trend for the medicalisation of death described earlier also gathered pace, notably in the form of vaccination, pain relief and germ theory. Death therefore was becoming more predictable, and when it did occur it was more often to be experienced as the natural conclusion of an increasingly long life. That said, the impact of social and medical developments during this period should not be overstated. Not far under the surface of apparent change and modern 'progress' the traditional understanding of an ongoing relationship with the dead, and sense of responsibility on the part of the living to see them safely into the after-life, persisted. This is especially apparent upon moving away from the urban centres, and into the Georgian and Victorian countryside.

A veritable catalogue of popular death portent beliefs, recorded by folklore collectors across England throughout this period, indicates that a good death was still, above all, an anticipated one. While many of these folk beliefs very probably were much older, and simply being recorded for the first time during the nineteenth century, the industrial age added its own superstitions. These included the belief that breaking a mirror would cause a death: since silver-glass mirrors were not mass manufactured, and therefore widely affordable, until the 1830s, this was merely a new permutation of the much older notion that death could be predicted. Similar can be said of the mantelpiece clock, whose ceasing to tick was also believed by some to signify a death in the offing.

For the upper social classes who could afford his attentions, the doctor became as much a deathbed presence as the priest – although in this period medicine's primary role was still to manage, rather than prevent death: what today would be called palliative care. The company of family and friends remained important: in the 1830s rural Yorkshire Dales, for instance, female neighbours would assemble at the house in a gathering called a passing. If loved ones could not be physically present at the deathbed, then the dying spirit might instead visit them at the moment of death. Funeral sermons continued to note approvingly when the subject had passed away peacefully, aided perhaps by the popular customs of removing bird feathers from the mattress, moving the bed from under a beam – or, indeed, moving the dying person from the bed altogether. Practical checks to ensure that the deceased really had died, and was not merely unconscious, could include placing a mirror or feather in front of the face to check for breath.

Immediately after a person had died it was customary to extinguish the fire in the death chamber, to cover reflective surfaces, and to open doors in order to allow the spirit passage without distraction or obstruction. The tradition of ringing the passing-bell upon a death also persisted late: in 1882 a Hampshire clergyman recorded a mother's being upset that her instructions to delay the ringing had been ignored, thus hurrying the spirit of her daughter Rosina out of this world. Although Purgatory very rarely received explicit mention by this time, there still persisted within these customs the sense of a soul or spirit requiring help to navigate its way from this world into the after-life. 'Telling the bees', popularly believed to be other-worldly spirits, of a death in the household and dressing the hives in black was another means of aiding the soul's transition into the after-life.

Another post-mortem event was the visit from the coffin-maker – or, increasingly, the undertaker – in order to measure the deceased for the coffin. Coffins during this period,

Anonymous artist's engraving of a woman 'telling the bees', c.1860s.

"TELLING THE BEES," BY E. K. JOHNSON.—FROM "THE ILLUSTRATED LONDON NEWS."

and well into the twentieth century, were constructed by hand. Funeral historian Brian Parsons recounts how elm and oak wood were the most popular materials, with some regional variations in preference. Pitch pine, Canadian light wood, walnut and mahogany also appear in undertakers' records. Aspen and alder were often used to make children's coffins. Once constructed the coffin was polished or varnished, or alternatively might be covered with white (for children), black or other dark fabric. The inside was also lined, while the outside was furnished with metal breastplate, handles and other ornaments of varying quality according to the coffin cost. Victorian coffins were considerably narrower than nowadays and had more sharply tapered ends, meaning that the deceased's arms had to be tightly crossed when laid inside.

Laying-out of the body at home remained important, and was carried out with care. The characteristics of both life and death were widely believed to be present during this in-between stage; there were folk beliefs that the dead could move around, and that a corpse could still sign a will if not yet cold. Sometimes food or drink would be left out for them. A 'penny for St Peter' (who traditionally holds the keys to Heaven) placed in the mouth or over the eyes, yet again indicates a lingering sense that the living owed assistance to the newly dead. Placing a saucer of salt (believed to have preservative properties and discourage evil spirits) upon the corpse's breast, was most often recorded in northern England and the Scottish borders, although there are occasional reports of this custom as far south as Somerset (c.1900) and Hampshire (1911). Candles would be placed around the corpse; while on a purely practical level they provided light, this practice may also have harked back to the medieval usage of candles as apotropaic devices to ward off the Devil and prevent the spirit from haunting the room. Other practices mentioned earlier, such as the covering of mirrors and other reflective surfaces to protect the living from accidentally glimpsing the dead soul, and suspending signs of life such as the fire or the ticking clock to encourage the spirit to move on their way, all point to a certain feeling of fear, as well as affection, toward the newly dead.

Similarly mixed feelings appear to have motivated the popular Victorian (and quite possibly older) custom of touching the body in order to prevent bad luck. In 1860 a young J.P. Emslie was taken to view the body of a recently deceased family friend, and years later recalled how his father had placed his hand on the corpse's forehead and told him to do the same. Part of the father's rationale was that 'they say that you should always touch any dead body that you see, for it prevents you dreaming of him at least.' Also notable here is the expectation children would participate as a matter of course, in contrast to nowadays. Such familiarity with the dead, and anxiety to be at peace with them, is better understood if we remember that this was still in the days before the funeral parlour, and when close physical proximity was unavoidable in often crowded homes.

The old tradition of waking also remained very much alive throughout the industrial period, despite the best attempts of Victorian funeral reform campaigners to eradicate it. As in previous times it performed the valuable function of providing the bereaved with an opportunity to reinforce the social and emotional bonds between its members, confirming, legitimising and alleviating the group's grief through collective performance of its shared memories. That said the obligation to host would also have been physically and emotionally intrusive – not to mention financially expensive – for the bereaved household, hence probably the eventual decline of this particular funeral tradition during the twentieth century.

Gold and enamel mourning ring, c.1780. Classical motifs such as this urn became particularly fashionable during the later eighteenth century.

The invention of photography in 1839 further illustrates how modern technology gave some old funeral traditions a new lease of life. The English had portrayed their dead in sculpture, drawing and paint for centuries, but photography made such portraits both more realistic and, as the technology developed, accessible to an ever-wider clientele. Photographers generally disliked the work, but recognised that it was lucrative: at least, as one remarked in a letter to a photographic magazine, the subjects could be guaranteed to stay still. Once taken these images would be kept and viewed within the family album, thus keeping the person alive in the collective memory. Here therefore we see modern technology affording increased expression to the age-old desire to commemorate the dead and maintain a relationship with them.

There was a huge proliferation of mass-manufactured funeral goods during this period: not only ready-made mourning-wear, but jewellery, stationery and even mourning tea sets were now available to any who could afford it – and to many who could not. Burial clubs, whose members made a small, usually weekly payment against the anticipated cost of such trappings, became increasingly common among the Victorian working classes and would eventually develop into the life insurance industry. When even this was unaffordable people exercised creativity, for example by dyeing existing clothes black or using the pawn shop as a clothing exchange. Contemporary funeral reformers (and indeed present-day historians) regarded such efforts negatively, as evidence of gratuitous consumerism and materialism; but an alternative reading is that industrial modernity was affording more people the opportunity to express feelings, bring communities together in the face of existential challenge, and, on a theme stretching back through time, to 'do right by' the dead.

Packet of funeral biscuits in printed wrapper, tied with black ribbon and sealed with black wax. These would have been doled out to relatives, friends and neighbours as part of the funeral bidding.

Ticket for the funeral of portrait painter Sir Joshua Reynolds, d.1792. Engraving by Francesco Bartolozzi after an original design by Edward Francis Burbey.

Another example of the care, effort and planning typically expended upon funerals during this industrial period was the system of funeral invitations, which had by now percolated right down the social scale. Folklorists recorded the custom whereby a 'bidder' wearing mourning would call at the houses of those invited to the funeral, bearing them a small printed invitation card. These cards were often accompanied by a packet of biscuits, or occasionally cake, wrapped in a black-edged paper printed with suitably reflective verses and sealed with black wax. Attending a funeral without having been thus invited was now an unthinkable offence against social propriety.

Heart-shaped wooden funeral biscuit mould.

Such preparations took time, and now the typical interval between death and funeral lengthened to over a week. During this interval the un-embalmed body shared space with the living as it decomposed, often occupying the family bed or table during the day while the children played around it.

The Victorian health and funeral reform campaigner Edwin Chadwick deplored how children of 'the labouring classes' were often left at home alone with the corpse, complete with maggots crawling on the floor, while their remaining parent was out making funeral arrangements. He blamed such situations upon a frivolous desire for social display, leading to delays in holding the funeral. While such comments may have contained a grain of truth, they also conveniently overlooked the practical realities for working people of overcrowded accommodation and a lack of safe, respectable alternatives for storing the dead. Furthermore Sunday was, for most working people, the day of the week available to hold or attend a funeral. Added to this was the popular fear of premature burial and the attentions of the 'sack-'em-up men', so that keeping the dead at home for an extended time remained almost universally traditional.

In another continuation from earlier times, mourners assembled at the house to share biscuits and burnt wine before the funeral. Even the very poorest would strive to provide a bottle of 'pooart' for the occasion. At a funeral in Market Drayton in June 1892 this ritual was performed in front of the local vicar, newly arrived in the parish, who expressed his disapproval of this 'pagan' custom and intention of putting a stop to it. Gloves, scarves and other gifts also continued to be distributed to funeral guests, with one Yorkshire vicar receiving sufficient scarves that his wife was able to make a dress from them. As in previous times the quality of these gifts was carefully graded

Guinea graves, Beckett Street Cemetery, Leeds. A social step up from burial in a common pauper's grave, this allowed the deceased to have some kind of permanent memorial – albeit one shared with strangers.

At the other end of the social scale, grand monuments such as these at Undercliffe Cemetery, Bradford, showcased the wealth and taste of the deceased and their family.

Coffin complete with light, oxygen pipe and alarm. Illustration from W. Tebb, *Premature Burial: How it May Be Prevented* (London: 1905).

according to the recipient's social status, so that the principal guests received kid gloves and the servants worsted.

Traditionally coffins were carried out of the house feet first, which was done in order to prevent the ghost seeing its way back. Rearranging the furniture while the funeral party was away was also believed to achieve this. In some parts it was customary for the coffin to then be deposited upon chairs or trestles, set up for this purpose outside the door, while the first verse of a hymn was sung. Further verses would then be sung – although it was no longer the practice to say prayers for the coffin's occupant – at intervals as the procession wended its way to the burial ground. As in previous times, sprigs of 'rosemary for remembrance' or other evergreen were often carried, to then be deposited in the grave. Although the medieval custom of

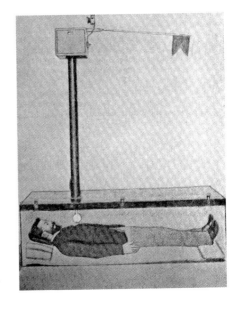

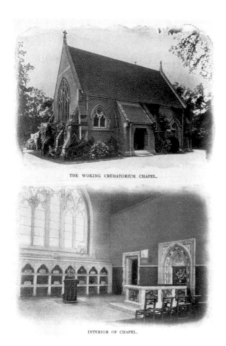

THE WOKING CREMATORIUM CHAPEL.

INTERIOR OF CHAPEL.

Interior and exterior of Woking Crematorium, 1909. By building crematoria in this ecclesiastical style, it was hoped to establish cremation as a respectable alternative to burial.

'giving dole' after the funeral service seems finally to have been dying out by this time, there are still occasional records of this being done into the industrial period. Instances of this include at Bempton, where in 1828 bread, cheese and up to ten shillings' (£30) worth of pennies would still regularly be distributed to the children and old women at funerals.

As in previous times, the funeral tea continued to be an important aspect of the proceedings – and to be criticised by reformers, who failed to grasp its importance as a means of social bonding following a rupture in the community. Thus food and drink continued to account for much of the typical expenditure upon funerals; for instance George Rhea, whose funeral tea in August 1846 included 10 gallons of ale, beef and ham, bread and £1 (£60) worth of cheese, as well as gingerbread, black and green tea, and 4lb of lump sugar. Although by this time funeral hospitality no longer carried a specific appeal for prayers for the deceased soul, there was still a strong desire to do right by the dead. This is apparent in the remark of an unnamed Yorkshirewoman, upon taking her leave after a funeral tea, that: 'You've done ivverthing by him you could; there's neea two ways aboot that!'

For those of much lesser means, a pauper burial on the parish carried increasing social stigma: 'only a pauper who nobody knows', as the saying went. Interment in an unmarked common grave, the norm for most previous generations of ordinary people, now became deeply shameful. One creative solution to this was the inscription or 'guinea' grave which, while shared with strangers, afforded at least an entry on a headstone. This desire to mark the existence of a named individual, and for some physical focus for a continuing relationship, found its fullest expression at the other end of the social scale, with large, elaborate memorials inscribing an individual's status, achievements, personality and relationships quite literally in stone upon the landscape.

With few reliable ways of definitively diagnosing death, the fear of burial alive was rife in Victorian England. This fear was expressed through popular culture, such as in Edgar Allan Poe's 1844 story *The Premature Burial*. The ever-inventive Victorians responded to this with a veritable armoury of devices incorporated into coffins: strings that pulled flags on the surface, bells, lights and whistles. However, there are no recorded instances of such a device actually ever having been activated.

As with the crematorium building, decorations illustrating Biblical scenes would have afforded this Victorian gilt pottery cremation urn connotations of tradition and respectability. Probably made by Davenport ceramic manufacturers, Staffordshire.

Under Christian influence, burial had been the normal method of disposing of the dead in England for over a millennium, but cremation now began to be mooted as an efficient, hygienic solution to the urban burial problem. The first recorded modern cremation was that of Honoretta Pratt of London in 1769; however, because cremation was so radically different it took until 1874 for the Cremation Society of England to be founded. Finally, in 1884 there came a crucial legal test case. On 14 January that year Dr William Price of Llantristant had cremated the body of his five-month-old son Jesu Grist, in full and deliberate view of people returning from evening chapel services. Cardiff Assizes eventually concluded that cremation was not, in fact, illegal under English and Welsh law. Thus it was that on 26 March 1885, at Woking Crematorium in Surrey, the body of Mrs Jeanette Pickersgill

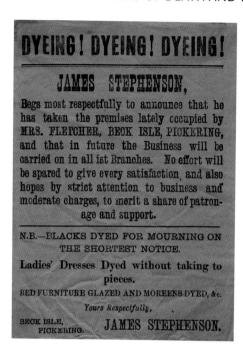

**DYEING! DYEING! DYEING!**

JAMES STEPHENSON,

Begs most respectfully to announce that he has taken the premises lately occupied by MRS. FLETCHER, BECK ISLE, PICKERING, and that in future the Business will be carried on in all ist Branches. No effort will be spared to give every satisfaction, and also hopes by strict attention to business and moderate charges, to merit a share of patronage and support.

N.B.—BLACKS DYED FOR MOURNING ON THE SHORTEST NOTICE.

Ladies' Dresses Dyed without taking to pieces.

BED FURNITURE GLAZED AND MOREENS DYED, &c.

*Yours Respectfully,*

BECK ISLE, PICKERING.        JAMES STEPHENSON.

Paper handbill by James Stephenson of Pickering, North Yorkshire, advertising fabric dyeing services. Dyeing existing clothes black for mourning was an economical alternative to making a special purchase.

became England's first legally sanctioned cremation. In 1892 Manchester was the first crematorium to open outside London, followed by Liverpool in 1896. The design of these early crematorium buildings deliberately resembled that of a parish church, with all its reassuringly traditional associations. In 1900, 444 cremations took place, a figure that had increased to 604 by 1905 and again to 1,279 in 1914.

Perhaps the best-known Victorian commemorative custom was that of wearing mourning clothes for a set period of time following a death in the family. Although the custom long pre-dated Queen Victoria, her wearing of mourning for Prince Albert (d.1861) was instrumental in making it eminently fashionable during the remainder of the nineteenth century and into the early twentieth. The custom found its fullest expression among the affluent middle classes who could afford to buy mourning clothes especially for the purpose, but those of more modest means found ingenious ways to adapt their existing garments. The requirements were most stringent for widows, beginning with a year in clothes draped with black crape, a type of silk crimped to remove all the softness and shine. After six months the amount of crape might be reduced. Mauve and other purples, grey or black-and-white half-mourning were permitted after another six months, although the truly respectable widow never wore colours again. The pressure to conform could be considerable: one young widow of a house painter, killed in the course of his work, purchased a full widow's bonnet complete with veil and streamers, after being told that refusal to do so proved the couple were never properly married. Men, however, were expected to wear only a black armband with normal clothes, highlighting again how the social and emotional work of maintaining relationships with the dead fell most heavily upon women.

Women were also prominent in the Spiritualist movement, which arrived in 1852. Although an American import, Spiritualism found fertile ground among the English. Its founding principles that the line between the worlds of the living and the dead was thin and porous, that the spirits of the dead continued to evolve post mortem and that they could share this knowledge with the living in an observable manner, perfectly combined a modern emphasis upon self-improvement and science with the age-old desire for continued bonds with the dead. The first Spiritualist temple opened in Keighley, West Yorkshire, in 1853, and the movement attracted followers from all walks of life from the working class to the aristocratic. Although a number of prominent mediums, including the Fox sisters themselves, were later exposed as frauds, the English continued to seek connection with their dead through Spiritualist rituals such as the séance. Interest in Spiritualism would peak during the Great War, and even nowadays there remain around 300 Spiritualist churches in Britain.

Popular keepsakes of the dead during this period included printed mourning cards, sometimes framed, mounted and displayed openly in the house; and also jewellery finely worked with the deceased's hair. By regularly looking at, touching and even wearing these items, people could reaffirm a sense of continued contact with their dead loved one.

SCARBOROUGH.

Postcard depicting a woman in mourning, c.1880. Her costume is fully covered in crape, indicating the deepest stage of mourning which lasted a minimum of one year for a spouse.

Mounted and framed memorial card for Ann Mortimer of Leeds, d.1864. Original background mount and slip supplied by J.H. Dale of Duke Street, Leeds.

Hairwork memorial brooch with 'in memory of' around the outside edge. Inscribed 'J. Oakley' on reverse.

Although mourning customs, and funerals in general at the turn of the twentieth century, were still elaborate by later standards, some historians have detected a change in mood beginning around 1860. Possible reasons for this include the efforts of funeral reform campaigners; but also, and more importantly in the long term, that life expectancy was slowly but surely increasing. Thus by the turn of the twentieth century death was becoming not so much the terror lurking round every corner, as the predictable, manageable culmination of a long life (at least in relation to the past). This in turn meant more opportunity to prepare, and correspondingly less acute need for elaborate, intensive funeral customs to navigate the associated social, emotional and spiritual rupture occasioned by death.

At this time these underlying cultural shifts were fairly gentle, and it's debatable

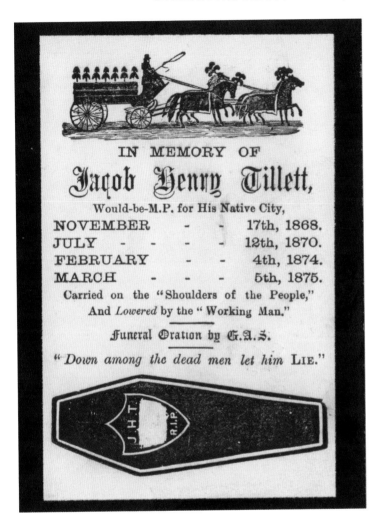

IN MEMORY OF

# 𝕴𝖆𝖈𝖔𝖇 𝕳𝖊𝖓𝖗𝖞 𝕿𝖎𝖑𝖑𝖊𝖙𝖙,

Would-be-M.P. for His Native City,

| | | | |
|---|---|---|---|
| NOVEMBER | - | - | 17th, 1868. |
| JULY | - - | - - | 12th, 1870. |
| FEBRUARY | - | - | 4th, 1874. |
| MARCH | - | - | 5th, 1875. |

Carried on the "Shoulders of the People,"
And *Lowered* by the " Working Man."

𝕱𝖚𝖓𝖊𝖗𝖆𝖑 𝕺𝖗𝖆𝖙𝖎𝖔𝖓 𝖇𝖞 𝕲.𝕬.𝕾.

" *Down among the dead men let him* LIE."

Memorial card for Jacob Henry Tillett MP (1818–92) of Norwich. Memorial cards were often distributed at funerals and kept as mementoes, with some examples as late as the 1930s.

how much people at the time would consciously have perceived changes to their own funeral customs and traditions. Traditional funeral customs, with their underlying belief that the living and the dead were intimately interconnected had, in their essentials, to a remarkable degree weathered not only the Reformation but also the challenges of the industrial age. War was just around the corner, however, and this would prove the greatest challenge yet to traditional English funeral customs.

# THE PRACTICAL DEATH, c.1900–2000

Graves of unidentified Great War soldiers at the Loos en Gohelle military cemetery, Pas de Calais, France.

THE YEARS FROM 1900 to the millennium, and especially the decades following the Second World War, have been characterised primarily by a *lack* of funeral customs and traditions. Medical advances, including notably the discovery of penicillin (1928), have combined with general improvements in living standards to steadily increase life expectancy. From 1948 this seemingly ever-improving healthcare became accessible to all through the new National Health Service. Since the mid-1950s more people in England have therefore died from cancer, heart disease and dementia – the chronic conditions of old age – than from the acute infectious disease. Indeed, the number of those surviving into extreme old age increased forty-fold over the century, from 75 centenarians per year during the 1920s to over 3,000 per year by 2000. This has radically altered experiences of dying – for the first time in history death became less the spectre lurking around every corner, and more the natural, and predictable conclusion to a long life fully lived.

The Blitz: several children were killed in this direct hit on a London school on 21 January 1943. Death on the home front, coupled with post-war austerity and profound social change, led many to favour a more practical approach to death and dying over the following decades.

As the twentieth century progressed other social and cultural changes also increasingly affected both people's desire and ability to maintain relationships with the dying and dead. Christian belief – especially belief in Hell – had already declined markedly by 1900, but secularisation gathered pace following the mass casualties of two world wars, and again as the richer, more individualistic 'baby boomer' generation came of age during the 1960s and '70s. As the spectre of post-mortem judgement thus receded, so did the perceived need to help the dead into the after-life. Instead the needs and wants of the living, especially those of the young, took priority. Families were becoming more geographically dispersed, while women – who traditionally performed most of the physical and emotional labour around death and dying – were increasingly working outside the home. Society generally was becoming more individualistic and materialistic. All these factors contributed toward the twentieth century's abandonment of many traditional funeral customs.

That said, bonds of affection and duty did continue to tether the world of the living to that of the dead. That was especially the case prior to the Second World War, when many traditional folk beliefs about portending death continued to hold. These included the beliefs that the clock stopping

Art Deco style brass coffin handle with associated Newman Bros. catalogue entry.

(Suffolk, c.1920), hair cuttings burning in the fire (Lincolnshire, 1932) and knocking sounds in the house (London, c.1940) were death portents. After the war, with death becoming ever more predictable and medicalised, and therefore generally less visible in everyday life, such beliefs saw a sharp decline; those that did linger often became softened to portents of mere 'bad luck'. For instance, in February 1966 the *News of the World* reported the coincidence of a woman's illness with her husband's bringing an injured starling into the house; in previous times his doing so would have been considered a death portent. Breaking a mirror or sighting a single magpie were other actions which also now portended bad luck, rather than a death. That said, such superstitions refused to die out entirely: the old belief that a howling dog portended a death persisted in Devon as late as 1971. Another one – notable especially given that by this time most deaths now occurred in hospital – was that the presence of red-and-white flowers in a hospital would cause a death.

Until the advent of the National Health Service most deaths in England still took place at home. In many coastal districts the folk belief that death could only occur at the ebb-tide lingered even beyond the Second World War. In 1920 J.W. Halton, Coroner for Cumberland (East Division) remarked how even the 'well-to-do' in his district still customarily covered the looking-glass following a death. Opening the doors in the house 'to let the soul out' was still being recorded well into the 1930s. And as late as 1963 a survey by anthropologist Geoffrey Gorer found that, particularly among the working classes and in northern England, window blinds were drawn for the entire funeral period. Some households even kept sheets especially for this purpose. 'Telling the bees' is still occasionally done up to the present day in rural North Yorkshire. By contrast the passing bell has mostly been silent since the Great War, forbidden from ringing by the 1915 Defence of the Realm Act.

The mid-1950s were a significant turning point in deathbed customs, since almost exactly half of deaths now took place in hospital. By 1965 hospitals and nursing homes accounted for 62 per cent of all deaths. While this development had the practical benefit of removing the nursing burden from families, it also effectively made redundant the traditional deathbed customs, which for many centuries had enabled final gestures of care and affection toward the dying person. Instead the bureaucracy of medical certification and registration now prevailed, with bodies being hastily removed by staff anxious to make space for the next patient. Thus the dead were now neatly tidied away, 'sequestered' to use the term coined by sociologists to describe how the later twentieth century preferred to ignore the dying and dead as an embarrassing failure of medical science.

Before the Second World War, and occasionally beyond, it remained customary to keep the dead person laid out at home in the traditional manner. As soon as possible the body would be straightened, sometimes with the aid of a communal laying-out board or even a door. Tying the limbs both made it easier to move the body, and reduced the possibility of the deceased 'walking.' The layer-out would wash the body with water and stop its orifices with

Shroud advert, c.1920s.

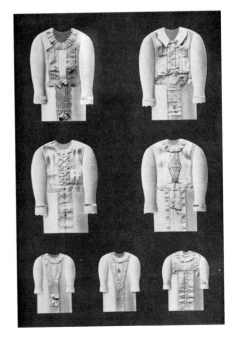

cotton wool, brush the hair and clean the fingernails. Men were shaved. A clean nightgown or shirt was then used to dress the body, although a prospective or recent bride might instead be laid out in her wedding-dress. Alternatively shrouds made of brushed cotton, linen or silk according to means could be purchased ready-made. From the 1970s a greater range of coloured shrouds became commercially available, enabling the deceased to be presented more individually.

*Two Mutes, photographed by Sir Benjamin Stone (1901). Common – in both senses – during the Victorian period and early twentieth century, these black-clad 'carrion crows' (Bertram Puckle) were rarely seen by 1930.*

The washed, dressed body was then placed in its coffin, with local convention varying as to whether the hands were crossed over the pelvis or chest. Blocks of salt or later dry ice, packed around the body, to some extent helped stay decomposition particularly in warm weather. If death had occurred in an upstairs room it was necessary for the loaded coffin to then be manhandled down often steep, narrow stairs. Historian Sheila Adams recounts how, in some unfortunate cases, the bedroom windows might even have to be removed to enable the coffin to be lowered in distinctly undignified fashion. Coffins at this time were heavier and more cumbersome than nowadays, being almost universally made of wood with metal fittings. Later on, the increasing popularity of cremation meant that lighter, more combustible materials were used in coffin construction.

Laid out in the front parlour with the window coverings drawn, traditional coins laid on its eyes and sometimes also a symbolic saucer of salt placed upon its breast, the body would viewed by visiting relatives, friends and neighbours keen to pay respects. At the turn of the twentieth century they might still have encountered a black-swathed mute posted at the door, although this particular custom was in decline and appears to have ceased altogether by around 1920. Throughout the inter-war period it remained very common for children to view the bodies particularly of other children. As adults, some recalled being compelled to touch the body and disliking the experience, while others enjoyed being given funeral cake upon visiting bereaved houses in the neighbourhood. Viewed from the perspective of the bereaved family, it perhaps was the intrusive, burdensome nature of these traditional visiting customs which contributed toward the growing popularity of the Chapel of Rest during the 1930s and beyond. Rather than being obliged to feed and entertain all and sundry who might appear at the house, the bereaved could now control access to the body and view it themselves in private at convenient times. Indeed, and as many people increasingly preferred, they might opt out of viewing altogether.

CHAPEL OF REST
"BUCKLEY CORNER"

DEDICATED BY THE LORD BISHOP OF WILLESDEN
1933

Promotional card for J. Crook's Chapel of Rest at Buckley Corner, Kilburn High Road, 1933.

The Chapel of Rest was also convenient in another very practical way, at a time when delays of well over a week between death and funeral were still commonplace. While this interval enabled relatives to be informed of the death and to travel for the funeral, many working-class homes still did not possess a separate space in which to accommodate a decomposing body. Although modern arterial embalming had been available in Britain since the early 1900s, it was usually impractical to carry out the procedure at a client's home and therefore not

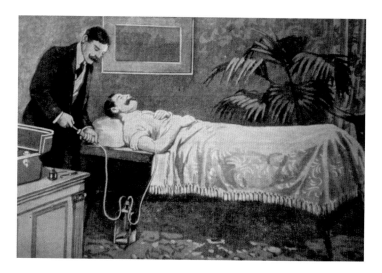

widely encouraged by undertakers. However, with the dead
now routinely removed to the undertaker's premises, usually
within a few hours of death, such 'hygienic treatment' could
be carried out much more easily. Therefore by the Second
World War, and in all but the most conservative communities,
the traditional ministrations of the female layer-out had been
almost entirely supplanted by those of the male undertaker
and mortuary technician.

Though burdensome and intrusive, traditional funeral
hospitality customs would have provided opportunities for
communal consolation and for coming to terms with the
reality of loss. With the body now abruptly removed as soon
as possible after death, traditional customs with symbolic and
emotional value such as keeping watch, placing candles and
suchlike became obsolete. Others, notably that of visiting to
pay respects, did continue to be observed, but in the absence
of the laid-out body lacked much of their former emotional
and social force. One woman, a teenager in early 1960s Leeds,
also recalled how such visits were carefully timed to avoid
mealtimes, expectations of hospitality by visitors having now
greatly reduced from earlier days. For those more socially

and geographically distant the sending of a sympathy card, produced commercially since the 1920s, became a practical means of expressing concern without the deeper emotional commitment of the traditional personal visit.

The customary method of bidding funeral guests also became considerably more practical, and correspondingly less personal, between the two world wars. This change was aided by technological developments, notably the telephone. One very late account of an old-style bidding comes from Upper Calderdale in Yorkshire, although with the custom described as 'dying out' by the time of writing in 1935. By this time it was rapidly being replaced by printed announcements in the obituary section of a local (or occasionally national) newspaper. These announcements were usually formulaic, and placed by the undertaker on behalf of the bereaved family. For those not already informed in person – the telephone only came into widespread domestic use during the 1970s – reading this announcement might also be their first news of a death. The announcement was generally understood to function as an open invitation to the funeral: the practical convenience of announcing a death in this manner overriding any desire to restrict attendance.

Funeral procession in Hammersmith, 1920s, featuring motor hearse and mourners' cars.

Practicality also increasingly prevailed when it came to departure for the funeral. In 1926 it was still customary in Catwick, East Yorkshire, to leave the door unlocked after a corpse had been carried out for burial to enable the spirit to depart; by the late 1940s such customs, which traditionally had marked the deeply symbolic moments of 'lifting' and departure, were all but obsolete. This was because the deceased had usually been removed to the undertaker's straight after death. Instead the coffin and its occupant, returned briefly from the undertaker's for this purpose, now arrived outside already loaded into the hearse. Consequently there was no longer a moment of final departure to be marked with special food and drink. Gift-giving customs were also now a thing of the past, and the house gathering was now limited to close family and occasionally selected friends. While this new way undoubtedly was more efficient – not least for the time-pressed undertaker – it also denied mourners the opportunity physically and symbolically to assist the deceased in moving on. The emotional punch of that final departure without looking back had been thoroughly pulled.

In 1933 *Folklore* journal reported that in Trentside, Lincolnshire, the old belief still pertained that the sex of the first

Funeral of Jim Lloyd, a former Battersea street trader, 1949. Note particularly the wreath-style floral arrangements which were customary in mid-twentieth century England.

person to meet a funeral procession determined the sex of the next person to die. By now, however, practical considerations increasingly governed the English funeral procession. The mass requisition of horses for the Great War coincided with the invention of the much cheaper, faster motor car, and by 1949 there remained only thirty horses left in the whole of London which were still regularly used for funerals. The motor hearse had arrived. That said, traditional horse-drawn, walking funeral processions were still occasionally to be seen, especially at working-class funerals and within particular communities such as the Pearly Kings and Queens of London. For most, however, the questions of who bore the coffin and walked behind were replaced by the question of who should have a sought-after place in one of the black cars which accompanied the hearse. All other mourners had to make their own way as best they might. The change from walking to motor funeral processions heralded shifts in other associated customs: for instance the carrying of herbs and flowers was replaced by purchased wreaths delivered straight to the funeral venue. The custom of singing along the processional route, meanwhile, was rendered completely redundant. The traditional corpse roads also fell out of use; only a few now survive and these mostly as heritage trails.

For the non-principal mourners, funerals during the second half of the twentieth century now began upon arrival at the church or crematorium. This group was increasingly less likely to include children, who by now were routinely excluded from attendance at funerals. At a church funeral it was and is customary to have arrived and be seated before the main party's arrival, as at a wedding. Meanwhile at most English crematoria, there was the awkward wait outside for the hearse and funeral cars to arrive, time which might be filled by inspecting the floral tributes – or even encountering the previous funeral. This was followed by an even more awkward, largely improvised and slightly hurried procession into the

Sutton Coldfield Crematorium, opened 1964 and typical of the 'domestic' style usually employed by later twentieth-century crematorium architects.

chapel. As demand soared crematorium funerals became strictly timed – 30 minutes including entry and departure was the norm. This allowed for little deviation from the Church of England order which, despite the fact of ever-decreasing church attendance, remained the standard funeral service. In the Reformation spirit this speaks about the deceased rather than to them, with mourners encouraged to mark a life already passed on 'somewhere' rather than any continued relationship.

In 1944 the Church of England formally approved cremation, with the Roman Catholic Church doing so in 1968. The latter was the same year in which cremation finally overtook burial in popularity. By 2000 242 crematoria were processing 75 per cent of English funerals. However tidy and quick it might be, however, the cremation process often left much unfinished in terms of human desire to relate emotionally to the deceased. Whether at the end the coffin was lowered upon a moving catafalque, shrouded by mechanically operated curtains or simply left standing in the chapel, the deceased was being abandoned to a mysterious process carried out by strangers behind closed doors. This imaginative gap became filled with persistent urban myths: that crematorium staff removed the bodies from the coffins which were then reused, or that the ashes of different people were carelessly mixed up for return to the none-the-wiser family. Traditions for the disposal of returned ashes also largely failed to become established, with some opting for burial and others for scattering, whether within the crematorium or cemetery grounds or at another personally meaningful place. Sometimes a bereaved spouse or family might retain the ashes at home as a way of maintaining their relationship with the deceased, but this usually was done discreetly so as to avoid accusations of being 'morbid'.

The funeral tea was one of the few traditional customs which persisted throughout the twentieth century, particularly among the working classes and in northern England. The foods served at a typical mid to late twentieth century English funeral tea – cooked meats and pastries, pies, bread and butter, cake – likely would have been eminently recognisable to a Victorian or even medieval mourner. While any notion of the funeral tea as a dole in return for prayers for the deceased had long since passed, even now there still remained a lingering sense of 'doing right by' them through the quantity and quality of food and drink provided for mourners. Before the Second World War and sometimes later, the food and drink typically was provided by the family and prepared and served at home by local women. Sometimes these were the same women who had also lain the deceased out. Since the War it has been customary instead for a hotel, pub or other external venue to be hired to provide catering.

The imperatives of efficiency also increasingly shaped burial customs during the twentieth century. Far fewer new cemeteries were opened after the Second World War, with government policy now prioritising land for housing and other facilities for the living. By the 1950s the cremation rate was already rising significantly, leading planners to assume that the need for new burial space would eventually peter out altogether. Meanwhile the tradition of regular visits to family graves was also in decline, leaving Local Authorities to assume the task of grave maintenance. Such new public cemeteries as were opened from the 1950s onwards were therefore mostly in the modern 'lawn' style, with regimented, standardised headstones designed more for ease of maintenance than for their consolatory value. Even here, however, small remnants of the older sense of connection with the dead have persisted, such as the popular belief that it is unlucky to walk over a grave. Meanwhile the filled-up Victorian garden cemeteries increasingly fell into neglect and decay, poignant physical symbols of weakened bonds between the living and the dead.

With the increasing popularity of cremation, there arose new commemorative customs. Or, perhaps, it would be more accurate to say that old commemorative customs took on new guises. Instead of graves, memorial plaques – which might or might not also be the disposal site of the ashes – started becoming the focus of memorial activity such as visits and the leaving of tributes. Another development was the crematorium 'book of remembrance', in which the name, birth and death dates of the deceased was recorded – the page then being opened annually upon the latter date, in a distinct if distant echo of the medieval year's mind. Lighting memorial candles is another very old English funerary tradition which continues to be popular.

The extended wearing of mourning clothes beyond the funeral, however, fell largely into abeyance during the twentieth century. According to costume historian Lou Taylor, Victorian strictures in this respect had in fact begun

Overgrown Victorian cemetery. With the income from new burials long since dried up, such sites are challenging for Local Authorities to maintain.

Memorial benches have been around since the late nineteenth century, but became especially popular from the 1960s onwards as people began seeking more personalised forms of commemoration.

to relax well before the Great War. In particular the practice of putting small children into mourning, except for very near relatives, was increasingly challenged from the 1860s onwards. A century later, by the time of Gorer's survey in 1961, only half of his widowed female interviewees wore any visible sign of mourning at all. By now a distinct social divide had emerged in this respect, with the older outward expressions of grief persisting longest and hardest among older people, the working classes and (again) in the north. On the whole, however, post-war England saw a growing culture of grief avoidance, and demand upon the bereaved quickly to cut ties with the dead almost as if they had never existed. The diaries of Dorothy Addison, widowed aged 55 in 1951, provide rare and poignant insight into the pain and isolation experienced by a mid-twentieth-century, upper-middle-class widow denied an ongoing social, spiritual or emotional relationship with a deceased beloved.

Within such an increasing atmosphere of death denial and avoidance, the medieval communal remembrance of All Souls fell sharply out of favour during the twentieth century, to be only partially replaced by the commercialised American import of Hallowe'en. Although Hallowe'en celebrates the

11 November 1922: crowds line Whitehall to watch the military ceremony commemorating Armistice Day around the newly built Cenotaph.

supernatural in a generalised way mainly aimed at children, the dead are not specifically remembered. Instead communal remembrance of the dead during the season of dying has, since the Great War, been dominated by Remembrance Day. At the official victory parade on 19 July 1919, the unexpected highlight was a centotaph to the fallen, erected temporarily for the parade. Such was its instant appeal to the bereaved public, individually denied the exercise of funeral customs by the wartime government's non-repatriation policy, that building work began immediately. On 11 November 1921 the permanent Cenotaph was inaugurated with a wreath-laying ceremony, and a two-minute silence observed throughout the country. This was accompanied by the burial with full honours of a purposely anonymous soldier, disinterred from the Flanders battlefield, in Westminster Abbey. The wreath-laying and silence are still repeated annually on 11 November (or since 1946 the nearest Sunday): it remains to be seen whether, and if so how this particular custom will further adapt in future as the two world wars recede further into history.

In terms of death in custom and tradition the period 1900–2000 has therefore essentially been a century of two halves, with the dividing line somewhere around the Second World War and a wider crossover period between roughly 1930 and 1950. Prior to this, mortality was still relatively high and unpredictable, death largely took place at home accompanied by traditional customs, and undertakers had yet to assume the role of funeral director. During the inter-war period innovations such as the sympathy card, motor hearse and cremation were steadily gaining popularity. Meanwhile old customs such as the passing-bell, mourning wear and All Souls were already defunct or in decline, as were all the traditional deathbed and laying-out customs now increasingly rendered redundant by the Chapel of Rest.

Following the 1939–45 war, there was a more decisive shift in favour of the practical, private death. The twin demands of institutional protocol and commercial interest subsequently came to dominate the process of dying from deathbed to committal, compounded by a culture which emphasised privacy and emotional control. Thus the decades from c.1950 to c.1990 were the apogee of the practical death: where the Protestant Reformation had previously failed, two World Wars and late-twentieth-century modernity would – nearly – succeed in estranging the dead from the living.

None of this, it should be stressed, had been imposed on an unwilling population. Innovations such as the Chapel of Rest and so on were in the main willingly, indeed enthusiastically embraced for the practical convenience, the privacy and freedom from burdensome obligation they afforded. Yet arguably something else was almost, and perhaps unintentionally lost along the way, and as the millennium approached the human need for continued bonds with the dead was already reasserting itself through new customs. Such new – yet also sometimes remarkably old – English funeral customs and traditions are the subject of the next, and final chapter.

# DEATH NOW AND IN THE FUTURE

AS THE TWENTY-FIRST century unfolds there is an increasing reaction against the institutional control, and practically convenient but emotionally unsatisfying funeral customs of the late twentieth century. Continued bonds between the dead and the living – and indeed the fact of mortality itself – are starting to be acknowledged again. The death and funeral of Diana, Princess of Wales in 1997 is often cited as a watershed moment in this respect, although influential celebrity funerals go much further back in history. From the 1980s onwards there have also been great numbers of 'disenfranchised deaths', notably victims of the AIDS epidemic who, rejected by mainstream society, were obliged to (re)invent their own funeral traditions. Meanwhile depictions of death, notably Damien Hirst's diamond-encrusted skull sculpture *For the Love of God* (2007), began re-entering the artistic mainstream for the first time in nearly a century, helping to re-normalise death in everyday discourse.

A straightforward return to old deathways would be impossible, however, since society and technology have changed considerably in the intervening years. In particular, English society is now far more individualistic and consumerist than at any previous time in history; and this applies as much to our relationships with our dead as to with one another. By the turn of the millennium, therefore, the dead were already re-exerting their claims upon the living in new – yet in some ways also strikingly old – ways; these are the subject of this final chapter.

OPPOSITE
Floral tributes to Diana, Princess of Wales, August 1997. Although royal and celebrity funerals down the ages have frequently been public spectacles, Diana's death and funeral are particularly credited with helping to break the English taboo around such matters.

An elderly inpatient. With average English life expectancy at 83 for men and 86 for women in 2018, social death nowadays often precedes physical death. For most of history this has been the other way around.

As matters currently stand, we all still have to die of something. For most people nowadays and in the foreseeable future, this is likely to remain the long, slow decline of cancer, dementia or another degenerative disease of old age. Sociologist Allan Kellehear argues that, far from improving upon the sudden death of old, this kind of death merely brings about its own variety of ambiguity and lack of control: the tedium and shame of a gradual, yet inevitable inability to function physically, socially and economically. Modern medical progress has gifted us more time to consider and to plan for the inevitable, but the need to do so firmly remains.

In this spirit of encouraging the English public to think and talk about this still-inevitable fact of life, September 2011 saw the country's first Death Café being held at the east London home of Jon Underwood. Based on a Swiss model, Underwood's aim was to provide an accessible, supportive and confidential space for members of the public to discuss death – their own and those of loved ones – informally over refreshments. This new custom of gathering to discuss death has since proved popular in the UK, with over 1,600 Death Cafés now operating across the country in cafés, private homes and other venues.

More formal ways by which an individual can set terms for their own post-mortem relationship with their survivors include making a will and the pre-paid funeral plan. Another related concept is that of death cleaning, in which the elderly systematically streamline the possessions accumulated over a lifetime, symbolically relinquishing the 'stuff' of life while reducing the burden on those who otherwise would be charged with clearing their material legacy.

Although traditional folk death portents as described in earlier chapters are rarely invoked nowadays, the notion that death can be predicted and even prevented still persists. For instance it underpins the public discourse of health and safety, with its implicit promise to prolong health and life. Faith in lifestyle habits such as diet and exercise is another example; ritual invocations of 'un/healthy eating' are arguably underpinned by the same kind of magical thinking which not so long ago made people reluctant to have may blossom in the house. Nowadays however, digital technology affords a means of individually quantifying these efforts to prevent death – apps such as Deadline: Watch your Life, Make it Count even promise to calculate a death date based on a combination of vital statistics and biometric data.

While such death prediction technology is currently in its infancy, it is likely to become increasingly accurate with time, raising the question of what customs and traditions will arise to help us cope with the social, emotional and legal consequences. One possibility is that euthanasia, or assisted suicide, may become more common. This is currently illegal in the UK, although there have been prominent campaigns for the 'right to die' at a predetermined time and in a manner of one's choosing. Experience from the Netherlands, where this is legal, suggests how custom and tradition might adapt if death were to become more predictable in future. There, the traditional funeral wake has made a

Since arriving in England in 2011, Death Cafés have provided a safe space to talk and think about death and dying.

comeback with a twenty-first-century twist – the presence of the soon-to-be deceased at their very own 'death day' farewell gathering of family, friends and neighbours.

Although most twenty-first-century deaths in England still occur in a hospital or care home, since the 1980s the hospice movement has attempted to combine the nursing care provided in such institutions with the traditional *ars moriendi* recognition that dying is more than simply a biological event; that it also involves a reconfiguring of social, emotional and spiritual relationships. An alternative, even more individualised way of assisting a dying person out of this world is to engage a 'soul midwife' or 'death doula' to provide emotional and practical support to the dying person and their carers. This title purposely invokes the traditional association between death and birth customs – although actual midwives have, at least officially, been prohibited from laying out the dead since the 1902 Midwives Act.

The immediate removal of bodies from their place of death to a Chapel of Rest remains customary. In fact it nowadays is so ubiquitous that this, along with 'hygienic' chemical embalming, is widely believed to be a legal requirement. While removal and embalming certainly have become customary since the 1930s, it nonetheless remains legal to keep the deceased at home with or without embalming. On a practical level, modern technology in the form of electric cool blankets now enables those who wish it to return to the traditional custom of keeping and caring for the dead at home for some or all of the time until the funeral. It is also sometimes possible for relatives and friends to be actively involved in washing, dressing and caring for the deceased at the Chapel of Rest. As these options become more widely known and taken up, customs and traditions to help the deceased and bereaved to move on emotionally and spiritually undoubtedly will (re) emerge; these are likely to include some revivals of certain very old customs, such as lighting candles around the body, together with other, new and perhaps digitally based traditions yet to be invented.

Modern technology is already enabling the revival of one old English funerary tradition: that of post-mortem portraiture. Having all but disappeared during the twentieth century, this custom is now making a comeback thanks to mobile camera phones. These permit high quality photographs of dead loved ones to be taken instantly and discreetly, with the resulting images easily shared via digital networks. 'Digital life tribute' services, which offer to combine photographs with other media such as home movies and music, already exist, and doubtless new (or reinvented) conventions will soon develop with regard to how, when and with whom such material is shared.

While it remains customary to place the deceased into a coffin for viewing and disposal, most twenty-first-century coffins are considerably longer and wider, with broader and less tapered ends than their Victorian or Edwardian equivalents. This allows for laying-out in a more natural, relaxed pose than would have previously been the case. There is also nowadays a greater range of coffin materials from which to choose to reflect the personality, interests and values of the deceased; from the traditional wood (effect), to the more artisanal wicker or cardboard – the Second World War cardboard 'utility coffin' perhaps an early precedent. Hand-decorating the coffin is something the bereaved can do for the dead, while facing the reality of events together. Meanwhile for ultimate individual expression in death, bespoke 'crazy coffins' embody almost any personal hobby or interest

Defiant black humour often features in the designs of 'crazy coffins', such as this example in the shape of a skip.

Triumph
Bonneville
motorcycle with
sidecar hearse.

from a ballet shoe or a sports bag to a canal boat. They also allow for expression of humour (see pictured).

Most of our dead are still disposed of with some form of accompanying ceremony. However in twenty-first-century English society the nature and form of this ceremony, and the relationships it expresses, is becoming increasingly personalised. Some take this individuality to its logical conclusion by opting out of tradition altogether, and having a 'direct' disposal with no service at all. Sometimes in these cases a memorial ceremony may be held at a later date.

For the majority who do still have a funeral in the conventional sense, transport remains a basic practical need, but nowadays many options are available to reflect the individual's personality, interests and tastes. Notable examples include a motorbike hearse (pictured), steam traction engines and a bright yellow three-wheeled car decorated with the logo of a popular British television comedy series. Even the old-fashioned horse-drawn hearse has recently been making a decided comeback – sometimes now in white or pink as well as traditional black.

Another twenty-first-century expression of individuality in death is to appoint a 'funeral celebrant' to tailor the funeral service to individual requirements. This means that the Anglican liturgy, not so long ago the universal norm, is now one among many options from which to select. Many funeral services nowadays blend religious, semi-religious and secular elements: according to a 2018 survey by one of England's major funeral providers, 65 per cent now include at least some element of personalisation. This often includes mourners wearing colours rather than conventional black, readings, and speeches by family and friends. It may even include the attendance of pets at the funeral. The advance of digital photography and home printing enabled personalised orders of service easily to be produced; these are often taken and kept as mementoes of the deceased, in much the same way as the Victorians kept mourning cards.

Flowers are still given and received at English funerals, although mourners less close to the deceased are nowadays often asked instead to make financial donations to a specified charitable cause. For those who do give flowers, the variety, colour and arrangement of these is often highly personalised. Examples given in the survey report included floral tributes depicting a favourite pet, football club badge or superhero character, reflecting the dead person's tastes and preferences. Alternatively, floral tributes might form a word expressing a relationship: 'mum', 'dad', 'granddad'. The old English custom of flowers at funerals has, it appears, adapted well to the age of the individual.

Music, another longstanding tradition, also continues to feature prominently in most present-day English funerals. However, this is another funeral custom that is adapting to the twenty-first century: nowadays one is as likely to find secular as sacred music being played. The Co-Op's 2016 survey of frequently chosen funeral music revealed an eclectic mix of religious and classical, pop and rock, TV and film pieces. These increasingly are played through devices (laptops, tablets, smartphones) supplied by the family – a further instance of mourners increasingly reasserting control of how the dead are sent on their way.

Funeral procession c.2015, including a modern twist on the traditional horse-drawn hearse and mourners dressed in football strip and casual clothing.

Humour is an important factor in musical funeral choices, with Monty Python's *Always Look on the Bright Side of Life* and Queen's *Another one Bites the Dust* receiving mention in the survey. Sometimes this music accompanies a slideshow of photographs of the

Personalised floral tributes.

deceased in various aspects of her/his life (post-mortem images normally remain private).

Sometimes, however, the role of new technology in funeral customs and traditions is more contentious. In particular, livestreaming of funerals over the Internet is now becoming more common. While this enables geographically dispersed family and friends to feel a sense of participation in the proceedings as they happen, for many people this emerging custom also raises serious questions concerning privacy and dignity. Similar questions surround other emerging customs: for instance, is it appropriate to 'check in' to a funeral on Facebook? To tweet the details of a funeral service as it happens? Or to take selfies at funerals (although research shows that most 'funeral selfies' are actually taken beforehand or afterwards, rather than at the service itself)? As in all the previous periods covered in this book, technology is constantly challenging and changing funeral etiquette.

Around 25 per cent of English funerals are still traditional burials. However, with most churchyards now full and closed, nearly all burials now take place in a cemetery. Graves are dug, usually by machine, by cemetery staff a day or two beforehand; grass mats placed around the grave opening on the day disguise the industrial reality of modern cemeteries. Sometimes the burial service – which may or may not be religious in nature – is read at the graveside, although the unreliability of British weather means that very often the service will have been held at another indoor venue. Thus many funerals are divided into two distinct parts of service and burial, very often with another journey in between. More recently it has become customary for the final committal to be restricted to family and very close friends – attendance at this part of the proceedings thus now a marker of the intimacy of relationship.

The ultimate way of managing access to a funeral and grave is to bury the deceased at home. Contrary to popular belief, home burial is perfectly legal in England provided environmental and general public nuisance laws are observed. Home burial remains rare in practice, given how the presence of a grave would likely impede the future sale of the house concerned.

Cremation is nowadays the majority option at just over 75 per cent, a rate far higher than in most of the rest of Europe. This raises the question of what then to do with the resulting ashes. One more recent form of holding – literally – onto the dead is to have the ashes made into jewellery, and a number of firms specialising in this new technology already exist. For most people however, the act of scattering of the ashes effectively becomes a secondary and final funeral. Like the committal of a burial service, this ceremony is generally private to a close circle of selected invitees. Scattering may take place in a designated area of a cemetery, or at another location meaningful to the deceased and/or bereaved. Due to the level of demand some locations now forbid the scattering of ashes, while in some especially popular locations (notably parts of the Lake District) the sheer volume of scattered ashes and associated litter is even changing the local ecology.

This, together with other concerns about the environmental impact of cremation, has prompted the invention of futuristic disposal methods such as resomation and promession.

The former, also known as water cremation, involves dissolving the body in a stainless steel container filled with water and potassium hydroxide. Heat and pressure then reduces the body to a liquid. Promession involves breaking the body down into a fine powder through alternately freezing and vibrating. Like cremation, both these essentially industrial processes lack the ritual drama and satisfaction of a traditional burial; however, they are relatively environmentally friendly, using less energy than cremation and with end products that nourish rather than contaminate the soil. This notion of an ongoing relationship with the living through giving, quite literally, of oneself back to the cycle of life, is currently most often expressed in the ever more popular trend for eco, or 'green' burial. While there is no fixed, legal definition of a green burial, it generally involves burial in a decomposable wicker or cardboard coffin with no permanent grave marker. In some respects therefore, this rather resembles the medieval approach to burial, although it is questionable whether the twenty-first-century bereaved actually experience this particular type of continued bond in the intended way. Certainly visitors to green burial sites often leave more conventional expressions of grief and memory, creating tension with others who prefer to maintain the natural aesthetic. Taking the logic of giving back to the natural environment even further, at the time of writing research into the practicalities of composting the dead is ongoing.

A further twenty-first-century development has been the legalisation in England, in 2010, of open-air cremation. The force behind this was Babaji Davender

Resomator. In a process sometimes called water cremation, this machine uses alkaline hydrolysis and pressure to reduce bodies to their component fluids

Olney Green
Burial Ground,
Olney,
Buckinghamshire.

Ghai, who wished better to facilitate the Hindu and Sikh belief in reincarnation; however, in so doing he also harked back to pre-Christian practice in parts of the British Isles. Open-air cremation using traditional wooden fuel has meanwhile also been (re)discovered in the United States, where it has been said to 'send off' the deceased in much more emotionally satisfying fashion than the modern industrial process.

Another futuristic body disposal option which alludes back to much older funerary customs has been proposed by the American DeathLAB: here the dead are placed in pods, which are then lit up by the bioenergy released by the decomposition process. To a historian this recalls the candles which, in English folk custom, used to be lit around the body at it was laid out at home. As decomposition completes over six to twelve months – recalling the timing of medieval and early modern minds, and also Victorian mourning stages – the light fades and finally goes out. At this point the remains are returned to the family for secondary disposal and the pod is then reused.

Whatever disposal methods become popular in future, and how this shapes the associated customs and traditions, the issue will be forced sooner rather than later. At the time

Cremator at Arnos Vale, Bristol. The first cremator in the West of England, this was opened in 1929 and operated until 1998. It now forms part of the cemetery's museum.

of writing some Local Authorities are already – whether knowingly or not – reverting to the medieval practice of reusing old graves due to lack of new burial space. There is also the related question of what to do with old, full legacy sites. Arnos Vale Cemetery in Bristol is a particular example of an old cemetery which has now become a heritage attraction and community space: perhaps in future it will become normal to visit a cemetery to eat coffee and cake, attend a yoga class or watch a film, as much as to mourn the dead; in the process arguably recapturing with a twenty-first-century flavour the community functions of the medieval churchyard.

Wayside memorials, where mourners place flowers and other items such as photographs of the dead person, soft toys and candles (again) at the site of death, have also become popular in England since the 1990s. These tend particularly to occur when the deceased is young and has died accidentally and/ or violently. Beyond commemorating a particular individual, wayside memorials often make a social or political point relating to the circumstances of that person's death, such as a protest against knife crime or speeding traffic. As well as being highly personalised, wayside memorials tend also to be more ephemeral than their traditional graveside counterparts, with only very close relations and friends maintaining them longer term.

People have decorated graves since time immemorial, but modern consumer culture has caused a proliferation of such items, including photographs, soft toys, statues, windmills and windchimes, bottles, balloons and LED lights. Such items are important to the bereaved, but present a major challenge for cemetery grounds staff.

In general, lighting candles as a way of remembering and connecting with the dead has remained a very popular custom down the ages. This can variously be done at home, at the site of death if accessible, at the grave or scattering site, in a place of worship or other place especially associated with the individual(s) concerned. Another, perhaps more surprising medieval survival (or revival?), is the custom of saying prayers for the dead. Davies' 2015 study of prayer requests collected at a major English cathedral found nearly half (42 per cent) of these requests were for prayers for the dead. Moreover, just over half of these requests were written as if directly addressing deceased loved ones.

To our ancestors the dead often lived on as ghosts, prompting as seen a range of magical customs aimed at helping their spirits to move on and limiting their ability to return to trouble the living. Not only does traditional belief in ghosts persist, sociologist Tony Walter has identified a new trend for people to believe that the dead become angels. Angels' duties have, as previously seen, traditionally included assisting the souls of the dead safely into the after-life; nowadays the dead are believed to *become* angels and are referred to as such on memorial inscriptions and online memorial sites.

Wayside
memorial, Bristol,
October 2018.

Another particularly twenty-first-century kind of revenant is the 'internet ghost' – the dead living on in cyberspace, popping up often unbidden to surprise and sometimes distress relatives and friends. Such reminders most obviously take the form of legacy material built up over the deceased's lifetime through conventional social media. There is also now a growing number of social media sites through which the dead continue actively to interact with the living through messages posted in advance. Certain social media sites can even be configured to post 'likes' calculated by algorithm on behalf of the dead; while some people might welcome this as a kind of digital immortality, to others this feels like a sinister appropriation of their post-mortem selves. Such services certainly raise the question of whether the dead have a right to decline continued bonds with the living, and be forgotten. The occupation of 'Digital Death Manager' has already sprung up to help people consider these questions and to curate their digital after-lives accordingly.

As life expectancy in the West has plateaued in recent decades, it's evident that death still remains very much a part of life. Funeral customs therefore continue helping us to accept and shape our continued social, emotional and spiritual bonds as with the dying and dead. Nowadays many of us aspire to negotiate such bonds as individuals, with customised funerals accordingly becoming more and more popular.

In a modern twist on the medieval belief that angels escorted the dead into Heaven, many people nowadays think and talk of their beloved dead becoming angels.

In practice, though, for all the rhetoric of choice many of us select remarkably similar personal touches to a ritual that has varied little in its fundamentals for centuries. Few are sufficiently brave to dispense with tradition altogether and be summarily disposed of as mere biological waste. Furthermore, upon examination many of these supposedly new funeral customs in fact turn out to be developments of much older ideas and practices. Perhaps it would therefore be more accurate to say that, as it has always done until now, death in custom and tradition continues dynamically to adapt to the times.

What will happen in the longer term, however, is much harder to say with any certainty. As we stand in the early twenty-first century Western medicine has now removed most of the biological barriers that previously prevented humans from living out their maximum natural lifespans. Any further gains in this respect are therefore most likely to come from artificial engineering of the human body to enhance both the quantity and, perhaps even more importantly, the quality of our natural lives. With organ transplants, artificial implants and performance enhancing drugs already routine, this invites profound philosophical and practical questions of what it will in future be to live – and therefore to die – at all.

# CONCLUSIONS

'$A$s we are, so you shall be.' Uttered by the ghosts of the three dead kings to their living descendants, these words are as poignant as when they were first penned by a fifteenth-century English priest. For all the promises of modern technology, death stubbornly remains an inevitable part of life.

The question, therefore, is not whether we face the uncomfortable truth of our mortality, but when and how we face it. According to some scholars, the entirety of human culture ultimately springs from a subconscious quest for immortality. We can certainly say that when faced with the process of dying, people in the past have come up with some remarkably creative ritual responses to this greatest of existential challenges.

Such customs and traditions have, at least on the surface, for the most part been of their particular time. In the Middle Ages, for instance, when little was known of human biology, to predict death according to whether the owls hooted or the cuckoos cried made perfect sense. In the increasingly digital world of the twenty-first century most English people rarely even hear an owl hoot or cuckoo cry; instead we place faith in the algorithms of an app which promises to use biological data in order to calculate our life expectancy. The means may have changed with the times, but the underlying desire to know the score of our years remains just as strong as ever.

Similar can be said of the customs and traditions surrounding the deathbed and laying-out. While English society has changed out of all recognition since the Conquest, with implications for where and when death typically takes place, the ideal (if not always the practice) of a 'good' death nonetheless has remained remarkably consistent down the ages. It is also still important for the dead to then be treated with as much care as circumstances and resources permit, to be washed, dressed and laid out.

Most English people – unless they deliberately opt out, or society makes a point of withholding a funeral – are still also disposed of in a way that fundamentally has changed little since the Conquest or even earlier. There is still a very practical need to transport the body to the place of disposal, which calls for both a suitably durable carrying box and a means of carriage. There is nearly always a carefully choreographed procession, which has several functions: it physically and symbolically moves the deceased on, advertises their and their family's actual or desired socio-economic status, and cements (or disrupts) social connections according to whom it includes (or excludes).

Not only does the funeral service itself move the deceased on socially, emotionally and spiritually, it sets the tone of future relationships between the deceased and their survivors. For several centuries the living and the dead were bound up in a web of mutual assistance: the living helping the dead through Purgatory with their prayers, while the dead interceded for the living back on earth. So powerful was this particular form of continued bond that, despite the best efforts of the Reformation, its legacy was still detectable in folk custom and belief nearly four hundred years later.

Except possibly for a brief hiatus during the later twentieth century, custom and tradition have also helped the English down the centuries navigate continued bonds with their dead well beyond the immediate aftermath. Whether by maintaining chantry chapels or making charitable bequests, by wearing mourning clothes or setting up a memorial website, these customs have helped reshape such bonds so that the relationship no longer requires the deceased's physical presence. Some other symbolism, notably that of light, recurs again and again in English funerary custom and tradition over time virtually unaltered. Continued bonds also operate at communal level, notably All Souls and more recently Remembrance Day.

When exploring death over almost a millennium of English custom and tradition, we should rightly be suspicious of naïve nostalgia. For instance it is common for historians and sociologists to criticise the Chapel of Rest as a modern abandonment of the dead; while conveniently forgetting what made it so popular in the first place. Yet, as the historian Julie Rugg notes, over time funeral customs have a remarkable way of coming back round to ever-so-slightly different places – as we are now seeing with the introduction of cool blankets enabling the dead to be kept at home again. This is just one example of how English funeral customs and traditions are themselves dynamic entities, which are sure to keep on living and changing long after we individuals have shuffled off our own mortal coil.

# FURTHER READING

At the time of writing there is a wealth of academic literature, together with an ever-growing number of popular books, on death, dying and funerals. The following list represents the best and most accessible, in the author's opinion, of both.

## BOOKS

Barnard, S. *To Prove I'm Not Forgot*. History Press, 2009.

Black, S. *All That Remains*. Doubleday, 2018.

Brandon, D., and Brooke, A. *London: City of the Dead*. History Press, 2008.

Curl, J.S. *The Victorian Celebration of Death*. Sutton, 2000.

Daniell, C. *Death and Burial in Medieval England 1066–1550*. Routledge, 1998.

Davies, D. *Death, Ritual and Belief*. Bloomsbury, 2017.

Doughty, C. *From Here to Eternity*. Orion, 2017.

Gittings, C. *Death, Burial and the Individual in Early Modern England*. Routledge, 1988.

Jalland, P. *Death in the Victorian Family*. Oxford University Press, 1996.

Jupp, P., and Gittings, C. *Death in England*. Manchester University Press, 1999.

Kellehear, A. *A Social History of Dying*. Cambridge University Press, 2007.

Linkman, A. *Photography and Death*. Reaktion, 2011.

Litten, J. *The English Way of Death*. Robert Hale, 1991.

Llewellyn, N. *The Art of Death*. Reaktion, 1991.

Magnusson, M. *The Gentle Art of Swedish Death Cleaning.* Canongate, 2017.

Parsons, B. *The Undertaker at Work 1900–1950.* Strange Attractor, 2014.

Richardson, R. *Death, Dissection and the Destitute.* Phoenix, 1988.

Rutherford, S. *The Victorian Cemetery.* Shire, 2008.

Scott, N.M. *The British Hearse and the British Funeral.* Book Guild, 2011.

Walter, T. *Funerals and How to Improve Them.* Hodder & Stoughton, 1990.

Walter, T. *What Death Means Now.* Policy, 2017.

Watkins, C. *The Undiscovered Country.* Vintage, 2011.

## WEBSITES

Association for the Study of Death and Society: www.deathandsociety.org

Calico: www.calicolabs.com

Commonwealth War Graves Commission: www.cwgc.org

Cremation Society of Great Britain: www.cremation.org.uk

Death Café: www.deathcafe.com

Dying Matters: www.dyingmatters.org

Folklore Society: www.folklore-society.com

Funeral Celebrants: www.funeralcelebrants.org.uk

Future Cemetery: www.futurecemetery.org

Good Funeral Guide: www.goodfuneralguide.co.uk

National Association of Funeral Directors (NAFD): www.nafd.org.uk

Natural Death Centre: www.naturaldeath.org.uk

# PLACES TO VISIT

*The Albin Museum*, F.A. Albin & Sons, Arthur Stanley
House, 52 Culling Road, London SE16 2TN.
Telephone: 020 7237 3637.
Website: www.albins.co.uk/who-we-are/#albin-museum
*Arnos Vale Cemetery*, Bath Road, Bristol BS4 3EW.
Telephone: 0117 971 9117.
Website: www.arnosvale.org.uk
*Beckett Street Cemetery*, 140 Beckett Street, Leeds LS9 7AA.
Website: www.beckettstreetcemetery.org.uk
*The Bone Crypt*, Holy Trinity Church, Squires Hill,
Rothwell, Kettering NN14 6BQ.
Website: www.rothwellholytrinity.org.uk/thebuilding.htm
*Boxgrove Priory*, Church Lane, Boxgrove, Chichester
PO18 0EE. Website: www.boxgrovepriory.co.uk
*The Cenotaph*, Whitehall, Westminster, London SW1A 2ET.
Website: www.britishlegion.org.uk/
remembrance/how-we-remember/memorials/
*The Chantry Chapel of St Mary the Virgin*, Chantry Bridge,
off Calder Vale Road, Wakefield WF1 5PL.
Website: www.chantrychapelwakefield.org
*The Coffin Works Museum*, 13–15 Fleet Street, Birmingham
B3 1JP. Telephone: 0121 2334790.
Website: www.coffinworks.org
*Holy Trinity Church*, 5A Priory Row, Coventry CV1 5EX.
Telephone: 024 7622 0418.
Website: www.holytrinitycoventry.org.uk

*Museum of Funeral History,* Thomas B Treacy Funeral
Directors, 29–31 Rosebery Avenue, Clerkenwell, London
EC1R 4SL. Telephone: 020 3797 4220. Website: www.
dignityfunerals.co.uk/funeral-directors/locations/england/
london/clerkenwell/29---31-rosebery-avenue
*Museum of London,* 150 London Wall, London
EC2Y 5HN. Telephone: 020 7001 9844.
Website: www.museumoflondon.org.uk
(War, Plague & Fire gallery)
*The Rosary Cemetery,* Rosary Road, Norwich NR1 4DA.
Website: www.friendsoftherosarycemetery.simdif.com
*The Spurriergate Centre,* St Michael's Church, Spurriergate,
York YO1 9QR. Telephone: 01904 629393.
Website: www.spurriergate.com
*Tewkesbury Abbey,* Church Street, Tewkesbury,
Gloucestershire GL20 5RZ. Telephone: 01684 850959.
Website: www.tewkesburyabbey.org.uk
*Undercliffe Cemetery,* The Lodge, 127 Undercliffe Lane,
Bradford BD3 0QD. Telephone: 01274 642276.
Website: www.undercliffecemetery.co.uk
*Victoria & Albert Museum,* Cromwell Road, London
SW7 2RL. Telephone: 020 7942 2000.
Website: www.vam.ac.uk
(Collection of Georgian and Victorian
mourning jewellery)
*The Wellcome Collection,* 183 Euston Road, London
NW1 2BE. Telephone: 020 7611 2222.
Website: wellcomecollection.org (History of medicine)
*Woking Crematorium,* Hermitage Road, St Johns, Woking
GU21 8TJ. Telephone: 01483 472197.
Website: www.thelondoncremation.co.uk

# INDEX